Nothing Spiritual about Chaos

Nothing
Spiritual
about Chaos

A practical guide for
Baptist church secretaries
and administrators

Rachel Tole

2000

Baptist Union
of Great Britain

Nothing Spiritual about Chaos

A practical guide for Baptist church secretaries and administrators

Rachel Tole

2006

Baptist Union
of Great Britain

www.baptist.org.uk

Produced on behalf of The Baptist Union of Great Britain
by Nigel Lynn Publishing and Marketing Ltd
106 High Street, Milton under Wychwood, Chipping Norton
Oxfordshire, OX7 6ET, United Kingdom
enquiries@nigellynnpublishing.com

The Baptist Union of Great Britain
Baptist House, 129 Broadway, Didcot
Oxfordshire, OX11 8RT, United Kingdom

British Library Cataloguing in Publication Data
Data available

ISBN-10   0 901472 82 4
ISBN-13   978 0 901472 82 3

1 3 5 7 9 10 8 6 4 2

Printed in the United Kingdom by
The Alden Group, Witney

Contents

Foreword

The church secretary has long played an important part in the life of any Baptist church, and if anything the role gets harder as the impact of greatly increasing legislation on charities increases, while the pastoral side of the job shows no sign of decreasing. Baptist associations and the national offices in Didcot have many resources which are available to Baptist churches, and the church secretary is also a vital link in ensuring that the church takes advantage of these resources.

Rachel Tole is very well placed to assist church secretaries in the task to which God has called them. She has not only been a church secretary herself (as was her father), but also serves as both association administrator and a member of many Baptist Union committees. She has therefore seen from many vantage points the breadth and depth of the role, and how much benefit there is to a church when the church secretary is functioning effectively.

Administration in a church, (and as you will see the secretary's role is much wider than administration), needs to be done effectively not as an end in itself, but so that the church can concentrate on its main objectives of ministry and mission. Church secretaries will find this book a helpful way to guide them in shaping the role that they have been called to fulfil, and of maximising the gifts they have been asked to share with the church for the Kingdom.

Philip M. Putman
Head of Finance and Administration Department
Baptist Union of Great Britain

Acknowledgements

Writing this book has been a joy and a privilege, but I couldn't have done it without the help and support of many people. So thank you to:

- the East Midland Baptist Association and, in particular, my friends and colleagues Peter Grange, Steve Mantle and John Bayes, for allowing me to take a three-month sabbatical in order to write it.
- friends and colleagues around the country – particularly Amanda Allchorn, Linda Holder, Karen Martindale, Hilary Treavis, Roger Barnett, Stephen Copson, Paul Goodliff, Chris Mepham and Philip Putman – who have offered me their support and encouragement, shared their knowledge and corrected my mistakes!
- Westdale Lane Baptist Church and, in particular, the three ministers I have worked with over the years, for allowing me to be me!
- my many 'role-models' including my father Gordon Ibbott, and Administry founder John Truscott.
- those ministers who gave me their insights on what makes a good church secretary.
- the many church secretaries, in the East Midlands and beyond, who helped with the research for this book and especially those who gave me their ideas on how to cope with the demands of the role.
- my husband David for his love, support and help with the proof-reading.

The cartoons on pages 13, 42 and 88 are reproduced by kind permission of CartoonChurch.com

Introduction

The changing role of the church secretary

In our (Baptist) denomination the office of church secretary is the most important lay office a member can hold. There is no other work which has so marked an effect upon the congregation, apart from that of the minister... The church secretary must be a man... working and administration. He must have an aptitude for administration, and be able to delegate work. He should preferably have had a good education, and have a certain facility of expression. He (or she) must have the full confidence of the whole church membership, and above all be a true servant of the Lord Jesus Christ.

So wrote Richard Fairbairn and Ronald Thomson in their 1965 booklet, The Church Secretary's Handbook.

The or she in the last sentence is the only indication in the whole booklet that the church secretary might not be male. This is not surprising, as in the East Midlands anyway, only about twenty per cent of Baptist church secretaries in the mid 1980s were female.

By the 1980s, when Fred Beacons Church Administration book was published, the proportion of female church secretaries had increased to around forty per cent. At this time the role of church secretary was, along with the church treasurer, still seen as highly influential. There may be others in the church who have stronger personalities, greater gifts and more Christian devotion, but these two – secretary and treasurer – are in greater position of power and, therefore, the progress of the church can be greatly affected by these important people (page 23).

Today (2006) things have moved on considerably. Around 60% of church secretaries are women and a number of churches have

1
Introduction

The changing role of the church secretary

> In our (Baptist) denomination the office of church
> secretary is the most important lay office a member can
> hold. There is no other work which has so marked an effect
> upon the congregation, apart from that of the minister.
> The church secretary must be a man of many parts, hard
> working and self-sacrificing. He must have an aptitude for
> administration, and be able to delegate work. He should
> preferably have had a good education, and have a certain
> facility of expression. He (or she) must have the full
> confidence of the whole church membership, and above
> all be a true servant of the Lord Jesus Christ.

So wrote Richard Fairbairn and Ronald Thomson in their 1965
booklet *The Church Secretary's Handbook.*

The 'or she' in the last sentence is the only indication in the
whole booklet that the church secretary might not be male!
This is not surprising as, within the East Midlands anyway, only
about twenty per cent of Baptist church secretaries in the mid-
1960s were female.

By the 1980s when Fred Bacon's *Church Administration* book
was published, the proportion of female church secretaries
had increased to around forty per cent. At this time the role of
church secretary was, along with the church treasurer, still seen
as highly influential. 'There may be others in the church who
have stronger personalities, greater gifts and more Christian
devotion, but these two – secretary and treasurer – are in greater
position of power and, therefore, the progress of the church can
be greatly affected by these important people' (page 23).

Today (2006) things have moved on considerably. Around 60%
of church secretaries are women and a number of churches have

appointed paid administrators to do some, or all, of the work previously done by a church secretary. Other churches have found it increasingly difficult to find someone to take on what can be a very demanding role, and have divided the workload among a number of people. It is, therefore, not so easy to write a 'one-size-fits-all' book about church secretaries as it was back in the 1960s!

My intention, however, in writing this book is to be a help and a guide to all those people who find themselves in some sort of secretarial/administrative role within their church and to do so in such a way that it will be relevant whether their church has five or five hundred members! So, as you read this book, you will probably come across things that are not applicable to your situation, but I trust that you will also find many things that are.

What is a church secretary?

Not an easy question to answer but here are three of the definitions that emerged from a recent training day for church secretaries in the East Midlands.

A church secretary is …

… the facilitator of the main purposes of the church.

… a curious blend of the spiritual and practical.

… a 'jack-of-all-trades' – willing to serve in all areas.

Each of these is a good definition but none of them is really complete in itself as they really refer to three different aspects of what it means to be a church secretary. The first is about what they actually do, the second is about gifting and the third is about attitude and character.

So, what do they do? Some churches will have a 'job description' for the role of church secretary – but not many! In most churches, being a church secretary is one of those things people are just supposed to know how to do.

In 1984, Fred Bacon listed six things that the church secretary's role should cover:

   1. Secretarial … e.g. filing, rotas, agendas, correspondence.

2. Organising ... e.g. church and deacons' meetings, Church events, Sunday services.

3. Acting as a consultant ... being a source of information about church life.

4. Publicising ... via notices, notice-sheets, magazines and notice-boards.

5. Delegating ... much of the above.

6. Pastoral caring ... especially of the minister.

Whilst this is a good way of looking at the role, I would like to suggest that, in essence, there are just three things that the church secretary should be doing – facilitation, communication and encouragement.

As mentioned above, one definition of the role of the church secretary is that they are the 'facilitator of the main purposes of the church'. There are two very important things to note from this definition. Firstly, that a church secretary is a facilitator – someone who enables things to happen. It doesn't mean they have to do everything themselves. Secondly, there is a reminder that all they are doing should be directed at helping the church to achieve its main purposes. In order to do that, of course, it does help if you know what the main purposes of your church are! However, those things that generally need to be facilitated within the life of the church is what the rest of this book is about!

The second key aspect of the role is communication. I could have just included this under facilitation, but I actually believe that this is one of the most important aspects of the role. Later on there is a whole chapter devoted to this subject, but for now, you just need to remember that, as church secretary, you should take responsibility for making sure that people know what they need to know!

The third aspect of the role is encouragement. A church secretary really needs to be a positive, but realistic, encourager within the fellowship. Specifically they should be a support and encouragement to the minister or lay-pastor. This is a key relationship which we will look at in more detail in a later chapter. One minister who has worked with a number of church secretaries said 'I look back with gratitude to those who saw it as part of their responsibility to care for the minister's well-being.'

However, being a church secretary is about more than what you do, it's also about the sort of person you are. In preparation for this book, I asked a few experienced ministers what gifts and qualities they had appreciated in the church secretaries they had worked with over the years. Here are some of their responses:

◆ Those I considered 'good' had the spiritual maturity to be church leaders rather than simply functionaries.

◆ An ability to keep confidences.

◆ High up on my list of priorities is humour and fun!

◆ A willingness to confront, not run away from, difficult church situations.

◆ A person of prayer and with a pastoral heart.

◆ Someone who is proactive and knows what they need to be doing but who keeps me informed (reminding me what I should be doing).

◆ Well organised, computer literate and has a good relationship with the church.

◆ Reliable and efficient.

I also asked them about the negative side and one minister responded with some suggestions of the type of people who, in his experience, don't make good church secretaries. He wrote:

Those not so good in this role fell into certain categories:

◆ The secretary who deep down wants to be the minister!

◆ The type who gathers too much by way of responsibility to him/herself and will not delegate.

◆ The morose, negative-thinking type, where everything you suggest has cold-water poured on it; very discomfiting, since secretary and minister normally work so closely.

◆ The headstrong, who act and then tell you afterwards!

◆ The 'shirty' who may be good administrators but are not 'people friendly'.

◆ The incoherent – those not able to express themselves clearly to others.

From both these lists you can see that a church secretary really needs to have spiritual maturity and good people-skills as well as having organisational and administrative gifts. In other words, they should be a 'curious blend of the spiritual and the practical' as one church secretary described herself.

If you are reading this book as a potential or newly appointed church secretary you may feel like giving up now – please don't! Yes this is a big job, yes it can all appear somewhat overwhelming at first, but remember that help is at hand. First of all, you are doing God's work and he will equip you for it. Secondly, the other leaders within the church should be a support to you in this role. Thirdly, you are part of the wider Baptist family and help is available in many ways through this. (For example, chapter 13 of this book includes advice from some experienced church secretaries on 'How to Cope with it All!') And fourthly, this book is intended to be a help – 'I only wish there had been some book like this when I took on the job' wrote one church secretary on seeing a summary of the contents. 'I had to learn the hard way.'

What do you do when no-one wants to be the church secretary?

This is not an uncommon situation and is one which many churches have had to face at one time or another. It can happen because the previous church secretary did the job so well that no-one else feels they could possibly do the same! It can happen because the previous person did such a bad job that no-one feels capable of picking up the pieces! It can happen because no-one feels they have the amount of time needed to do the job! Or it can happen simply because no-one wants to do it!

The best solution is to divide up the role between a number of people. Ideally, though, someone should still have the title of church secretary even if much of the actual work is done by others.

Here are some ways this can happen:

1. A church secretary is helped by others such as –

   A **minute secretary** who takes the minutes for church meetings and deacons' meetings. They could also have responsibility for copying and distributing them as appropriate.

   A **pulpit supply secretary** who books all visiting preachers and deals with related correspondence.

   A **membership secretary** who is responsible for keeping the membership list up-to-date, producing contact lists and overseeing the membership application process.

2. A secretarial team of two or three people divides all the work between them according to their gifts and/or available time. One of them is officially the church secretary and their name appears as such in the BU handbook and elsewhere. This person will receive all the official correspondence. The team will need to meet regularly to make sure everything that needs to be done is being done. In this scenario, one person might have responsibility for everything to do with church and deacons meetings; another might have responsibility for internal communication – notices and notice-boards and rotas – and another is responsible for correspondence and booking visiting preachers. Other jobs are then shared between them as they arise.

3. Appoint an administrator – paid or unpaid – to assist the church secretary. How the work is divided up will depend on the size of the church and how much time is allocated to the administrator. In a small church with a part-time unpaid administrator working from home, they may simply be responsible for typing and photocopying the minutes, church magazine, notice-sheets and rotas. In a larger church, a paid administrator in a church office will do those things, manage the building and liaise with groups using it, type the correspondence for the minister, oversee all publicity, deal with health and safety issues, liaise with visiting preachers, buy all the supplies (tea, coffee, paper, cleaning materials, stamps etc.) and much, much more besides.

This is not an exclusive list but it does give some ways in which churches have solved the 'no-one wants to be the church secretary' issue.

There are also some Baptist churches who no longer have anyone with the title 'church secretary'. Here are just three examples.

Barrow Baptist Church in Leicestershire has between 140 and 150 members. They are fortunate to have found someone who has the gifts and the time to take on the roles of both church secretary and church treasurer. He has the title 'Church Administrator', is unpaid and spends between twelve and sixteen hours each week on this work. A similar situation exists in some small churches where the same person is both secretary and treasurer. In a smaller church however, especially if there is no paid minister, then the work can be done in much less time!

Sutton Coldfield Baptist Church in the West Midlands has over 500 members and a full-time paid administrator who fulfils the traditional roles of secretary and treasurer and also has responsibility for the management of the building, human resources and legislation issues (plus a few other things!).

Queensberry Street Baptist Church in Nottingham has between 140 and 150 members and no church secretary or administrator. Instead they have a full-time 'Development Co-ordinator'. About one-third of her job description is administration – mainly week-to-week stuff such as the notice sheet and some correspondence – and the rest is youth and church development. Other aspects of the church secretary's role are spread among the church leadership – e.g. pulpit supply and taking minutes.

In the end, each church will need to come up with its own way of making sure all the various organisational and administrative tasks that need to be done are done. If your church needs some help in finding a solution to the 'No-one wants to be the church secretary' problem then contact your local association. They may be able to point you in the direction of other nearby churches which have faced similar issues, or someone from the association may be able to come to the church and help you work out the best way for your church.

2
The Gift of Administration
A Personal Reflection

What do you think of when you hear the word 'administration'? For most people the word conjures up negative images – something that is necessary but rather tedious and boring. Now I used to think like that!

I remember many years ago filling in one of those 'discover your gifts' questionnaires and discovering that my main gift was administration. I was really disappointed – why couldn't I be like the other people in the group who had pastoral or teaching or preaching gifts? Administration sounded really boring and definitely un-spiritual. But then I made some important discoveries ...

Firstly, I changed from using the *Good News Bible* to the *New International Version* and discovered that in that version, administration is both biblical and spiritual! In 1 Corinthians 12.28, in the list of people God has appointed in the church, there are 'those with gifts of administration'. So now I knew that administration was definitely biblical and, as it's listed between healing and speaking in tongues, it would appear to be spiritual. That was quite an important discovery for me and I think it's an important thing for churches to grasp as well. Too often church administration is seen as un-spiritual and that is a great mistake.

Secondly, I discovered that the Greek word that is translated as administration is *kubernesis*. This literally refers to the work of a pilot who steers a ship through the rocks into harbour. Now *kubernesis* isn't always translated as 'administration' – in other versions of the Bible you will find 'governments', 'those who have power to guide others', 'those who can get others to work together' and 'organisers' (amongst others). Many of these indicate that *kubernesis* is really about leadership – but I still think that we can apply this to church administration.

Those people in a church who have the gift of administration are those who can help steer it through various practical obstacles to reach its goal. When I realised this, it was something I could start to get enthusiastic about. It's much more exciting than what most people think of when they talk about 'admin' – filing, writing minutes, drawing up rotas. Now all those things have to be done, but if you start to see them as part of helping a church to reach its goal or fulfil its mission, it can make them seem a little less boring!

Different people will have variations on this gift – some will be strategic planners and thinkers, some will easily see how to organise things so they happen quickly and efficiently and others will just get on and do the things that need doing in order to help the church achieve its mission. All churches need good administration if they are to do more than just survive and so those people who have administrative gifts are crucial. Everything that happens in a church needs organising and there is nothing spiritual about chaos.

What really made the difference though, as far as I was concerned, was the definition given to me many years ago by the minister with whom I was working. When he told me I had the gift of administration, he said that meant that I was capable of 'seeing needs, finding solutions, organising resources and developing structures'. As far as I am concerned this is what administration is really all about and it's what I have tried to do both as a church secretary and in the jobs I have had as an administrator.

I was also helped in my early days in administration by the existence of an organisation called Administry. Sadly this is no longer in existence but its founder, John Truscott, is now working as a church consultant and trainer and has a really helpful website (www.john-truscott.co.uk). For some reflections on administration as a biblical theme have a look at Training Notes TN21 in the resources section of his website. As he says in his introduction to the paper, 'Administration is a gift of the Holy Spirit to the church. It's a ministry that serves all other ministries. The words "administration" and "ministry" share a common root.'

So don't let anyone ever tell you that administration is unspiritual, boring or irrelevant!

3
Communication

This is one of the most important aspects of the role of church secretary – making sure that people within the church, and outside, know what they need to know. So much of what goes wrong within the church stems from poor communication – people grumble because they 'don't know what's going on', others feel hurt and ignored when they aren't consulted about something that will affect them, rumours circulate rapidly and church members stay within their own little cliques – and that's on a good day!

So what should be happening, and what role does the church secretary need to play in all this?

The notices

One of my abiding memories from growing-up in a church where my father was the church secretary was his reading of the notices each Sunday. These were methodically prepared, using the notices book produced by the BU for this very purpose, and carefully read out. For some church secretaries this is still a key part of their job but, if we are honest, it's not usually the most inspiring part of the service.

A large number of churches now have printed notice-sheets and it is the job of the church secretary to either produce these or make sure that the necessary information is passed on, in good time, to the person who is doing so.

Often, those churches who do have printed notice-sheets find that important information has been missed out and/or items need highlighting and so end up having to give out a version of the notices anyway.

And still people within the church say that they don't know what is going on!

So, here are some ideas on how to make the notices a little more effective.

- Ensure that printed notice-sheets are clear and easy to read. Don't use a multitude of different fonts or clutter them up with lots of clip-art! Make sure the things that people need to respond to in the near future are obvious and not mixed up with general on-going notices.

- Having a lot of verbal notices in addition to a printed notice-sheet is not a good idea. If, however, there are things that need to be highlighted, then try and find someone with good communication skills to do this – and someone who is enthusiastic about the item that needs to be highlighted.

- If you are reading out the notices you may find that a lot of the things you are reading out are the same every week. If this is the case, then maybe you could simply refer people to somewhere else where this information is available – church magazine, list on a notice-board or something else.

- Have different people read the notices each week – maybe share this among some of the deacons. This will mean not only a change of voice but also, maybe, some variation in presentation style, all of which will mean people are more likely to listen.

- If you use a data-projector, then have a 'notices-loop' which is projected as people arrive, over coffee at the end and, possibly, at some point during the service as well.

- Plan ahead! Because not everyone is at church every Sunday, you will need to advertise events several weeks ahead.

- Make use of e-mail. You could have a list of people who would like the weekly notices sent to them this way. This means that if they are unable to be at church one week they can still be kept in touch. Also, people who have sight disabilities and use a computer will be able to read a notice-sheet much more easily if it is sent to them by e-mail

◆ Instead of having a notices slot during which many people simply switch-off, have a 'family-news' slot (or slots) which can include some notices. If this slot also includes prayer for the things that have been shared then this will have a side-benefit of reinforcing the notices!

Notice-boards

Be creative with the various notice-boards you have inside – and outside – the church.

OUR SERVICES ARE A BIT DULL AND NOT MANY PEOPLE TURN UP, WE DO NOT HAVE A WEBSITE AS WE DO NOT REALLY KNOW HOW TO MAKE ONE, AND THERE IS NOT ANYONE AVAILABLE TO SPEAK TO YOU AT THE MOMENT AS WE ARE ALL QUITE BUSY, WHAT WITH ONE THING AND ANOTHER

PS WE NEED SOME MONEY FOR THE ROOF

WE DO NOT NEED TO GET SOMEONE IN TO HELP US WITH MARKETING OUR CHURCH AS WE ARE PERFECTLY ABLE TO DO IT OURSELVES

A notice-board outside can say a lot about your church and so, if you have one, it's absolutely vital that it's up-to-to-date and relevant. A good way to check out how this is perceived is to ask people outside the church what they think about it. If you use a notice-board to advertise special services or events then someone needs to have the job of removing posters as soon as the event is over. Posters advertising something that happened days, weeks, or even months ago, simply reinforces the view that the church is 'behind the times'. If you use the board to put up posters aimed at non-churchgoers then they need to be used carefully. Sometimes these 'words of wisdom' are not that wise at all and can be a bit of a turn-off for non-Christians, so you might find it helpful to have some feedback on these.

Now take a look at your internal notice-boards. Are they attractive or cluttered? Whom are they aimed at? Does anyone actually read them? I used to be fairly cynical about notice-boards and had the opinion that if you didn't want people to know about something just put it on the notice-board! But then it was pointed out to me that there are people who do read notice-boards – visitors! Parents waiting for children to finish in youth-club or Brigades may find their eyes drawn to a notice-board or other display in the area they are waiting. New people to the church who have stayed behind for coffee but don't know many people to talk to will drift towards a notice-board for something to do. In what ways could you use your notice-boards for the benefit of these people?

If you have a major project in hand, or particular event coming up, then you can use a notice-board as a special focus to update people on progress being made. Using large wording that people can see from a distance will draw people towards your board. Pictures, a '…. days to go' poster and frequent references to our 'special-project' board will remind people of its presence and encourage them to keep looking.

You may also like to designate one or more of your notice-boards to specific groups within the church to display pictures, craft-work, prayer requests etc.

Whatever you use your internal notice-boards for, make sure that someone has the job of checking them over regularly – removing out-of-date posters, replacing missing drawing-pins, tidying them up and generally making them as attractive as possible. This person – in consultation with the leadership – should be the only person allowed to display notices on the boards. This will prevent them becoming cluttered or even being used by individuals to promote their own hobby-horses.

Newsletters and magazines

Most churches will produce some sort of monthly publication such as a newsletter or magazine. If yours does then there are two key questions which those involved in producing them should know the answers to – '**Whom** is it for?' and '**What** is it for?' Even if the answers were clear when the magazine or newsletter was started, these questions should be reviewed regularly. The answers will help determine the content, presentation and language of the publication. If you also have a weekly notice-sheet, then there needs to be clear co-operation between the people producing both publications.

This book is not the place to look in detail at the technicalities of writing, layout, editing and production. These are covered in a booklet called *Getting the Message Across* by Richard Littledale and published by BUGB. Although technology has moved on since this was written, the basic principles still apply.

Websites

More and more churches now have their own websites and, when done properly, these can have a very positive impact. However, a poor website will reflect badly on your church. It may stop people from ever visiting the church and can reinforce the stereotype that the church is out of touch and irrelevant.

So, if you are going to have a website, you need to recognise that this is a long-term commitment. Apart from the time taken to decide what to include in the first place, your webmaster will need to update the site regularly, and also look for ways to change and improve it.

Be very careful about what information is put on your website. Names, addresses, 'phone numbers, e-mail addresses and photographs of individuals should only be included where those individuals have given their permission – and even then with caution. Pictures of children should not generally be used and names and other details of children should definitely not be given.

The *Useful Resources* chapter at the end of this book has some websites which give helpful advice on creating a church website.

Special presentations

From time to time within the life of the church there will be the need to communicate something special. This may be in a service or at a church meeting (or both) and could relate to any number of things such as a planned outreach event, visit of a prospective new minister or the need to make a major decision in the life of the church. Time spent in preparing for this will be time well spent.

Firstly, decide what you need to communicate and try to reduce it to a core message – a one-sentence summary. **Secondly**, you need to try and put yourself in the shoes of the rest of the church – how will they react to what will be said? This isn't always easy particularly if the leadership had been working on this matter for some time. **Thirdly**, you need to decide what outcome you are looking for – prayer-support, people to come to an event, volunteers to commit time to a project or whatever.

You can then work out what needs to be said – avoid too much detail or too much information which will prevent the core message being heard. Think about the order. Do you have the time to spread this out over a number of weeks, adding to the information given each time?

Once you have done that then you can look at ways of putting over the message – verbal presentation, PowerPoint®, drama, notice-boards, take-away leaflets, etc. Think about whether you are the best person to do this. What is needed – authority, enthusiasm, good communication or technical skills? Should you involve others either in the preparation or the presentation?

And, once you have done it, ask for some feedback from people who will be lovingly honest with you!

And finally … if you want to explore this subject further you may find John Truscott's *Ten steps to help you communicate* (TN2) helpful. This gives a checklist of issues to consider when preparing any item of communication and can be found in the resources section of his website (www.john-truscott.co.uk).

4
The Church Meeting

Most church secretaries spend a fair amount of their time on meetings within the church – both church meetings and deacons/leadership meetings. This isn't surprising as church meetings are a significant feature of life in Baptist churches.

The church meeting 'is the occasion when members come together to prayerfully discern God's will for their life together. In Baptist churches the final authority rests not with the ministers or deacons but with the members gathered together in church meetings. It is the church meeting which, for instance, appoints ministers, elders, deacons, and others who exercise various forms of leadership within a local congregation, agrees financial policy and determines mission strategy.' (From the 'What makes a Baptist' page on the BUGB website.) For those who would like to think more about this aspect of Baptist life, I would recommend Chapter 6 of *Radical Believers* (revised edition, 2006) by Paul Beasley-Murray.

The church secretary has an important role to play before, during and after every church meeting and, although some of it can be delegated, it is still a significant part of the role.

Before the meeting

Firstly, you will need to let people know the meeting is happening! Ideally a list of dates of church meetings should be produced annually and circulated to all members. Your church's constitution and rules will also indicate how much notice needs to be given for each meeting. Normally the minimum requirement is that the date, time and place for the meeting are publicised at the worship service(s) on the previous two Sundays. You will need to make sure that this happens.

Secondly, an agenda will need to be prepared and, ideally,

publicised beforehand. This will normally be done in consultation with the minister or whoever is chairing the meeting. Church meeting agendas will vary considerably and so it is impossible to give a definitive model agenda that will work in every church.

It is important, however, to remember that church meetings are not simply business meetings but are about prayerfully discerning God's will together. This means that prayer and worship should be key features of the agenda. The meeting will invariably start with worship or opening devotions and often close with the Grace – but there should also be opportunities for prayer within the meeting as well.

When preparing an agenda …

1. Remember to read through the minutes of the previous meeting to see what needs to be followed up in this one.

2. Be clear in your own mind about why each item is on the agenda – is it for information only, for general discussion or will a decision need to be made at the end?

3. Make sure you know who will be presenting each item – and check that they are aware of this as well!

4. Have some idea of the amount of time needed for each item.

5. Think about whether the order is logical. Are there some items that need to come before others?

It is also useful to have an agreement within the church as to who can put items on the agenda. Should everything come through the deacons or can any church member ask for a particular issue to be raised? Some churches will have a deacons' meeting a couple of weeks before the church meeting to agree what will be discussed at the latter.

It is a good idea to publish the agenda before the meeting. This can be done in a number of ways – putting it on a notice-board on the preceding Sunday and drawing people's attention to it; having copies available for any member who would like one; providing a named copy for every member and circulating it to them all (some could be done by e-mail). The best way for your church will depend on a number of factors, not least the size of the membership and the time and resources available. The disadvantage in providing an agenda in advance of the meeting is that people may decide not to come if it doesn't look very interesting! However, I believe that this is outweighed by the fact that some people will come to the meeting having given some prayerful thought to the items being discussed.

Note that for a Special Church Meeting you *have* to let people know in advance what is on the agenda. (See later section for more on this.)

And finally, as you prepare for the meeting check that you have everything you will need. Even if there isn't a ballot vote planned it is still a good idea to have a supply of small pieces of paper just in case someone suggests there should be one! The BUGB model constitution, for example, says that 'If not less than three members request a secret ballot for a vote on any matter then a secret ballot shall be held'. If you need to have a certain proportion of the membership present in order for the meeting to take place, then make sure you know what the current membership of the church is. It is also a good idea to make sure you have a copy of the church's constitution and rules with you.

At the meeting

Traditionally the church secretary will sit next to the person chairing the meeting and make sure that they know what they should be doing, and when! If you have a minute secretary, then it is still a good idea to make brief notes on your copy of the agenda which you can refer to later. Your role throughout the meeting is one that you can develop over time with the minister (or whoever is chairing). This can include such things as giving agreed signals when you feel things should be moving on. Many ministers also appreciate someone sitting with them to act as a sounding-board if things get a bit tricky. If possible you should take time occasionally to discuss with the minister how the two of you can best work together during church meetings.

If you don't have a minute secretary, then you will need to take notes through the meeting, making sure that you accurately record the wording of decisions that were taken. If you are not clear as to the exact wording then ask. It may well not have been clear to others either and that could only lead to arguments later on. For formal proposals note the names of those who proposed and seconded the motion and record the voting figures where relevant.

Your church's constitution will tell you what proportion of those voting must agree for a decision to be valid. In some churches this will be a simple majority – in others it may be two-thirds or three-quarters. Although it is the responsibility of the chairperson to ensure that these have been achieved, you should also check the figures.

You may have to present items at the meeting – look at the 'special presentations' section in the chapter on communication for some advice on this.

After the meeting

You have two responsibilities after a church meeting. One is the production of the minutes, and the second is to make sure that all the actions that were agreed are carried out. You should aim to produce the minutes within a few days of the meeting and there are some good reasons for this. Firstly, you will find it easier to decipher your scribbled notes whilst you still have some memory of the meeting. Secondly, you will be able to clarify the actions that need to be taken as a result of the meeting. Hopefully, you will not be responsible for actioning everything, but you do need to check that those people who have agreed to do something, do it!

Writing the minutes

The minutes of a meeting are a record of the decisions that were taken. Their purpose is to give an accurate account of what was agreed and how the decisions are to be implemented. It does also help to have some explanation of how a decision was arrived at. However, they are not a verbatim account of what took place.

Some churches may still be using a church minute book with handwritten minutes but most will be using word-processors or computers to produce them. Minutes produced in this way should, once they have been signed as a correct record at the following meeting, be kept in a suitable ring-binder and stored carefully.

Some helpful hints ...

- ◆ Keep them short and succinct – a lengthy discussion should be summarised in a couple of sentences. The minutes of most church meetings should be no longer than two sides of typed A4 paper.

- ◆ Keep them clear and easy to read by making good use of short sentences, clear headings and sub-headings, numbered points and gaps between items.

- ◆ Don't use people's names in a description of a discussion. This is likely to cause problems at the next meeting when people either complain that they have been misquoted or that you ignored their comment!

- ◆ Summarise the discussion or argument by saying something like 'During the discussion, two main points emerged: (1) we should retain our evening services, and (2) there needs to be greater variety within the services to attract more people.'

- ◆ Do use a spell-checker and ask someone else to proof-read them once you've finished and before they are copied.

The question then arises as to what you do with the minutes once you've written them. Again, the answer will vary between churches.

Some will do nothing with them until they are read out at the next meeting. This is usually the case where the minutes are handwritten and not easy to photocopy. However if it is possible to provide a copy for the minister in advance of the meeting then this is helpful.

Reading out minutes can be very time-consuming, and so many churches will circulate copies of the minutes in advance of the meeting. Where possible, they should be given to every member (or every 'active' member) – some could be sent by e-mail.

The timing of when they are circulated is a matter of judgement. If it is done shortly after the meeting then that is helpful for those who weren't able to be present. On the other hand, a lot of people will lose them before the next meeting. Most churches who circulate minutes will do so with the agenda of the next meeting. If you do this, you could also have some copies available earlier to give to those who weren't able to be at the meeting. In the end, each church has to work out what works best for them.

Special Church Meetings and Annual General Meetings

Special Church Meetings are held, for example, in order to call or dismiss a minister or to close the church! Other reasons for a Special Church Meeting will be in your church constitution and rules. The main difference between an ordinary and a special meeting is that you do have to tell people in advance the reason for the meeting. Sometimes you will also need to give a longer period of notice – three Sundays instead of two for example.

Minutes of the previous meeting and any other business should not be on the agenda of a special meeting as the meeting has been called only to deal with those items specified. You can, however, hold an ordinary church meeting straight after a Special Church Meeting has been concluded.

The Annual General Meeting is, in essence, no different from an ordinary meeting. It's just that the agenda usually includes annual reports and elections, unless, of course, your constitution says otherwise!

Chairing the meeting

Although this is not normally the responsibility of the church secretary, some will occasionally find themselves in this role. Note that, if this is the case, it is vital that someone else takes the minutes. Chairing a meeting is not an easy task but you may find the following helpful. It has been adapted from an article written by John Truscott and used with his permission.

The person in the chair is responsible for:

1. **C**larity – helping people to understand what a particular item is trying to achieve and where the meeting has got to on a particular item.

2. **H**armony – not the same as unity! This can be helped if people understand the business to be done, respect the leadership of the person in the chair and listen to and trust each other.

3. **A**greement – if a decision needs to be made, then the person chairing needs to make sure the meeting does just that. Timing is important – do things too quickly and people feel cheated – do it too slowly and many feel frustrated.

4. **I**nvolvement – the size of the meeting will determine the best way to achieve this. Obviously in a church meeting of 150 people you can't allow everyone to have their say – but you can if they split into smaller groups for part of the time. Even in small meetings there will be people who talk a lot and others who say nothing. Those who chair these need to be proactive in bringing everyone in. This calls for sensitivity in handling quieter members and firmness in dealing with the zealous talkers.

5. **R**eview – not included just to provide an R for the mnemonic, but because this is a vital part of the work of any group who want to improve their meetings. Take time to ask (of yourself and others) what lessons can be learned and what could be done better next time.

If you want to learn more about chairing meetings then John

Truscott has two articles on the subject in the resources section of his website. They are A5 *How to chair meetings* and TN13 *A purpose statement for those who chair*.

Decision-making

The actual processes involved in making decisions can cause conflicts within church life. Whilst the responsibility for this doesn't really lie with the church secretary, some awareness of what can help to make things easier could be useful.

The Fit4life material (see Resources chapter) has a whole section on 'Healthy decision-making' and using this could be helpful for any church where this is an issue. Having used this material in training events I have evolved my own **six principles for good decision-making**.

1. **Allow time and space for prayer and reflection** – so don't rush into things! Provide opportunities for God to speak to you as individuals, as a leadership and as a church.

2. **Actively consult with those likely to be affected** – a lot of problems can occur in a church when people think they've been overlooked. Don't make assumptions about what people think – ask them!

3. **Allow alternative possibilities to be considered** – the first solution you think of is not always the right one. If, like me, you think that you always have the best ideas, then you may need to exercise some grace and humility and actually listen to the ideas that others have.

4. **Provide an opportunity for discussion without decisions** – sometimes church meetings can get hijacked by people who want the church to make a decision quickly. But people need time to think things over and, ideally, important decisions should be raised at one church meeting and a decision made at the next one after people have had time to think, pray and talk about it – and have some of their questions answered.

5. **Make sure there is a clear recommendation** – another reason things can go wrong is because people aren't

24

clear what they're being asked to decide. Sometimes this happens when various side-issues are raised and people are then confused. Sometimes it can happen because the person bringing the recommendation is rather vague. So, if you are bringing a recommendation to the church meeting, be clear about what you are asking people to decide.

6. **Ensure good communication throughout** – let the members know what they are going to be asked to decide in advance of the meeting if at all possible. Sometimes it can be helpful to let the members know if the leadership is working through a particular issue. They are then able to offer prayer support and may also have some insights to share.

And finally … there are more ways to find out how people feel about a proposal than simply taking a vote. Try the 'spectrum' approach when facing a major issue. The idea of this is to find out how strongly people feel about an issue. Just because the majority vote 'yes' to something doesn't mean they are all 100% behind it.

There are two main ways of using this spectrum approach – one is public and the other private. For the public version you ask people to arrange themselves in a line across the room where one side is 'Yes, yes, yes!' and the other side is 'Over my dead body!' You can use appropriate words to indicate where people might stand such as the ones above plus 'Good idea but I can't get involved', 'Totally undecided', or 'I'm not convinced – yet!' – or numbers to indicate a range from 100% for to 100% against.

The private method allows people to do this along a line on paper. With both methods you can ask people to express their feelings at the start and then move their position (physically or on paper) after the discussion or time of reflection. Which method is most appropriate will depend on a number of factors including the size of the group, relationships within the group and the issue under discussion. Obviously this is not a proper vote but it may help the leadership see what people are thinking and decide what work still needs to be done before a formal proposal is put.

5
Ministry

Most churches have someone who has been called by them to serve as their minister or pastor. They may be full-time, part-time, ordained, a lay-person or a student training for the ministry. The relationship between that person (or persons if there is more than one) and the church secretary is a key one and so I have devoted a whole chapter to the subject of ministry within Baptist churches.

There are, however, some churches who have no-one in this role. Where this is the case the church secretary will usually have more of a leadership role than is the norm. If you are in this situation then it is vital that you have people you can call on for help and advice. These should include the regional ministers in your association and ministers of nearby churches.

Whilst the rest of this chapter is mainly aimed at those churches who normally do have a minister or lay pastor, this doesn't mean that it is irrelevant for the others.

How to cope without a minister

Ministers leave churches for all sorts of reasons! The most common reason is that they have received a call to another church or ministry and, generally speaking, the church secretary is the first person to know about this. If you have had a good working relationship with the minister, then he or she may already have talked to you about their decision to move and you may also decide together the best way to inform the church of this decision. Sadly, however, it doesn't always work like that and you may only find out at the same time as the rest of the church. Normally speaking a minister will have to give the church three months notice of their intention to leave.

Another reason for leaving a church is that the minister is retiring. This may be because they have reached retirement age or are having to retire early on health grounds. In these circumstances you will probably have known about this for some time.

The first thing you should do, once you know that your minister is leaving, is to make contact with your regional minister. Some associations have a regional minister with specific responsibility for ministerial settlement. Others have divided this work among their regional ministers on a geographical basis. Throughout the search for a new minister your regional minister will be available for advice and to provide information concerning prospective ministers. However, this is not a process that should be rushed into, as the focus during the notice-period should be on enabling the present ministry to finish well.

The second thing you should do is to get hold of the BUGB publication *Facing a Pastoral Vacancy*. Your regional minister will provide a copy for you, or you can order it from Baptist Publications or via the website – www.baptiststore.co.uk

The third thing you should do is plan for your minister's leaving 'do'. This may be a special service, a party or both. Even if there is sadness because of the imminent departure of the minister and often a family as well, there is usually much to look back on and celebrate.

However, some ministers do leave churches for less-than-positive reasons. This might be because of financial reasons, a breakdown of relationships between minister and church or because the minister has had to resign owing to 'conduct unbecoming to the Baptist ministry'. In these cases the likelihood is that you will already have been in contact with your regional minister for help and advice as this will be a very difficult time for the church. If not, then you should make contact as soon as possible. In these circumstances a 'leaving do' might be inappropriate but you may like to discuss other possibilities with your regional minister.

The fourth thing you should do once you know your minister is leaving is for your leadership – deacons and/or elders – to look together at the practical aspects of running a church without a minister. Many tasks fall to the minister of a church so during a vacancy these will need to be done by others. It is the responsibility of the church leaders to see to these things, although that does not mean they have to do it all themselves! The *Facing a Pastoral Vacancy* book mentioned earlier looks at these in some detail but as a summary the main things the leaders need to consider are …

1. **Sunday Services** – finding people to lead worship and/or preach. These may be people from within your own church or from the wider church. Your association may be able to help by providing a list of lay-preachers in the area. Having someone other than the church secretary organise this is advisable as there will be many other things for the secretary to do during the pastoral vacancy.

2. **Pastoral Care** – If you already have a pastoral care team then, after liasing with the minister before s/he leaves to make sure no particular needs are missed, they should be able to continue the work they were doing anyway. If no such team exists then one of the leaders should take responsibility for overseeing this work. It may then be a good idea to set up a team of people to visit regularly those who are housebound or who have specific ongoing needs. More specialised care may require help from other local churches or ministers.

3. **Mission** – this shouldn't stop just because the minister has left! Again, it will be helpful for one of the elders/deacons to keep an eye on this.

4. **The Manse** – if you have one – will need looking after. You may want to consider letting it. If so, then your first step should be to obtain the Guidelines Leaflet (A5: *Letting a Manse*) from the Baptist Union Corporation. This is also available as a download from the BUGB website.

5. You might like to think about appointing a **Moderator** as experience has shown that churches who do have one during a pastoral vacancy greatly appreciate the help and support they provide. A moderator is someone, usually a minister of experience, who will at least chair all leadership and church meetings relating to the pastorate.

Such a person may also be able to do some preaching and cover pastoral emergencies or 'specials' like baptisms and weddings and offer pastoral advice and care to the leadership team. Your regional minister can help you find someone suitable who will then need to be appointed by the church meeting on the recommendation of the leadership.

For many churches the main issue during this time is the call of a new minister and this will be the subject of the next section. However, this is not something that should be rushed into and, in most cases, should not really be discussed until the previous minister has actually left!

How to call a minister

As mentioned above, the person who will be the greatest help to you in the search for a new minister is your regional minister. They will normally start by meeting with the leaders and outlining the processes involved. Before you start the process you should also check your trust deed as it may require the church to have an accredited minister of the Baptist Union. Ultimately, under God, churches may call whoever they decide to be their minister, but if this means stepping outside the provisions of the trust deed, then a 'waiver' will need to be obtained from the church's custodial trustees. Your regional minister can help you contact the right people. You should also note that, at present, Home Mission grant-aided churches can only call accredited ministers.

If you are in an LEP (Local Ecumenical Partnership) then there will be special arrangements for seeking a new minister and these will be set out in the church's constitution. As well as your regional minister, your county ecumenical officer will be able to give you help in this area.

The following is a **summary** of what is involved in calling an ordained Baptist minister. Much more information is contained in *Facing a Pastoral Vacancy* including a suggested pattern for a church profile, recommended terms of settlement and questions to ask prospective ministers. Note that if you are looking for other forms of ministry such as a lay-pastor, the process will be different but you should always start by discussing your situation with your regional minister.

1. Prepare a church profile which you will eventually send to prospective ministers. This should let them know what you are like as a church now, what you believe to be God's vision for the church and the sort of ministry you are looking for. This profile should be agreed by the whole church.

2. Provide an eighty-word summary of your church's profile to be included on the 'pastoral vacancy list' which is sent monthly to all ministers seeking a pastorate. Ministers can ask for their name to be sent to any church on this list, so it can be seen as a limited form of advertising.

3. Make a decision about who within the church will take responsibility for finding a new minister. In some churches it is the deacons, elders or both who will have this responsibility. In others a 'search committee' is appointed which includes some leaders and others from the wider church. In the latter case, any prospective minister may well want to meet with the deacons (or equivalent) as well to see how that group works.

4. Meanwhile, all ministers who are seeking a new pastorate will have been asked to prepare a personal profile which gives details of, among other things, their personal gifts and skills, theological principles and previous work experience.

5. The National Settlement Team – which consists of the regional ministers who have responsibility for settlement – meets most months. They have the profiles from all ministers looking for a new pastorate and students leaving the Baptist colleges. Following the meeting, your regional minister will send you a number of profiles from possible ministers which they believe are worthy of prayerful consideration.

6. The profiles should be photocopied and circulated to all members of the 'search group' a few days before they meet. The best time for this group to meet is about a week after the Settlement Team has met. The group should then prayerfully look through the profiles to see which, if any, the group would like to meet with. It is important to remember that this is a confidential process and the names given to the group should not be disclosed to anyone outside the group at this stage.

7. There will then follow a period of meetings and visits and more meetings and more visits, and often a chance for a prospective minister to lead worship and preach, until the 'search group' feel that they have found the person they believe God is calling to lead the church. This person will then be invited to 'preach with a view to the pastorate'. This visit should also include time for the church to meet informally with the minister.

8. A Special Church Meeting will need to be held to consider calling a minister and the church rules should be checked to make sure the correct procedures are followed. Ideally it should be held in the week immediately following the prospective minister's visit. The minister should be informed of the decision without delay and an invitation to the pastorate given, if that was the result.

9. If the invitation is accepted you will need to agree with them when the announcement can be made public and celebrated.

10. You will then need to finalise the terms of settlement, agree a starting date and plan the induction service! This should also be done in liaison with your regional minister who will normally conduct the act of induction. (Two suggested service outlines for an induction are included in the BUGB book *Gathering for Worship*.)

As part of the discussions with a prospective minister the issue of housing is sure to have been raised. It is normal for a church to provide a manse for the minister and his/her immediate family.

If you don't have a manse, or the one you have is not suitable for the needs of the new minister, then you will find the BUC Guideline leaflet A2 on buying a manse invaluable. Sometimes a minister and church will jointly own a manse and sometimes the minister will own his own home. BUC Guideline leaflet A4 gives details of both of these options. Whilst the church treasurer will usually take the lead in these matters, it is helpful if the church secretary also has some understanding of what is involved.

You may also find it helpful to discuss with the new minister whether he or she will work from home or need office space at the church, or both! There are good arguments in favour of any of these options and ministers will differ in their opinions. A good minister will take advice from the leadership as to what might work best. Of course, in some situations there is no space in the church building for an office.

How to work with a minister

As mentioned in a number of places in this book, the relationship between minister and church secretary is a key one. Of course, like all relationships, this needs willingness on both sides to make it work! But even if it is hard going at times, do all that you can to keep the lines of communication open with your minister or lay-pastor.

Fortunately, most ministers will appreciate the help and support of their church secretary. This is indicated by the responses I received when I asked a few ministers about the church secretaries they had worked with over the years. 'A church secretary who is able to reflect with me creatively on issues and situations is invaluable' wrote one, and another mentioned the importance of 'offering support through good and bad times'.

Obviously you will have to work out the best way to nurture this relationship in your own situation, but here are some thoughts.

1. Remember that no two ministers are alike and the way you worked with one minister will not necessarily be the same as the way you work with another. Similarly you may have to remind your minister gently that you are not the same as the last church secretary s/he worked with!

2. Make sure that you keep each other informed of what is happening and avoid taking decisions unilaterally. Regular meetings together (maybe with the treasurer as well) for prayer and discussion about church life are very helpful. These meetings will help to build a collaborative relationship that will be very beneficial to the church.

3. Be a friend! 'The church secretary should keep a watchful eye on the minister, to make sure his or her spiritual and other needs are being met, being ready if necessary to give some gentle but firm counsel, for example, about taking time off' said one minister and I think many would agree with him. If a church has elders, then they may see this as one of their responsibilities but this shouldn't mean that the church secretary isn't involved in caring for the minister as well.

4. Be open and honest with each other. There may well be times when you have to say things that are hard for a minister to hear. This will be easier if you have built up an open, honest and, above all, caring relationship. One minister mentioned that one of his worst experiences was when a church secretary 'kept quiet about potential problems out of deference to my "feelings" until things got to crisis point'.

5. Talk about how you will work together in church meetings. Decide how, and when, you will put together an agenda. If the minister is chairing these, what sort of help would s/he like from you? Find out if they would appreciate an advance copy of the minutes.

6. Support each other if things get tough. 'After one particularly hard church meeting the church secretary put her arm around me and prayed for me; that was Christian love in action' recalled one minister. (On a personal note I greatly appreciated the flowers that my minister sent me after a very difficult church meeting when I was church secretary.)

7. Whilst it is important to have a good relationship with your minister, make sure it remains an appropriate one.

How to help someone who feels called to the ministry

The last section in this chapter gives you some idea of what you will need to do if someone in your church feels that God is calling them to become a Baptist minister. There are a number of steps that they will need to take to confirm this calling and there are ways in which the church can help in this process. It is helpful if you, as church secretary, are aware of this process so that you can provide some help and support for anyone making this decision. At the time of writing, the Baptist family trains and accredits people for pastoral, evangelistic and youth ministry.

The first step is for the person (the 'candidate') to discuss the matter with their minister. If the church has no minister then they might find it very helpful to discuss things with the minister of another local Baptist church.

The candidate will then need to make contact with your regional minister, who will be able to advise them on the next steps they will need to take. They will also be there to guide and support them and, where appropriate, their spouse, through the whole process.

An important part in this process is for the church of which the candidate is a member to indicate that they believe God is calling them to become a Baptist minister – be that pastoral ministry, evangelistic ministry or as a youth specialist. This is done at a church meeting, where the candidate has the opportunity to share with the church what they believe God is calling them to do. The meeting should then prayerfully consider whether this person has the qualities of character, leadership, spiritual experience and gifts that indicate they are being called by God into full-time Baptist ministry. If the decision is positive, then a letter of commendation should be sent to the regional minister, or be given to the candidate for them to include with their application. If the decision is negative or unclear, then the minister or church secretary should contact the regional minister to explain why the church meeting felt unable to commend the candidate.

Once the church has commended a candidate they will need

to be interviewed by the association's Ministerial Recognition Committee so that the call can be tested by the wider Baptist family. As part of this process the candidate will be asked to supply names of people who could give references and, as church secretary, you may be one of these. If you are then you will be sent a form to complete and may also be asked to comment on a service that the candidate has led.

If the association commends the candidate then they can be interviewed by the Baptist college(s) to which they have applied. They will also have to undertake a medical examination. If both of these have a positive outcome then they will begin a three or four-year training course at the start of the next academic year. The 'home church' would want to support them throughout their time at college. This can be done through prayer, encouragement and, if appropriate, financial help. Increasingly, however, many candidates follow a church-based pattern of training which will mean they become the student minister of another church and effectively move away from their home church. The home church will have to think about the best way to support them in this situation.

If a candidate has already reached the required academic level through previous study or training then they may not need to undertake further training. In this case they will need to attend the Baptist Union's Residential Selection Conference which will have the final say on whether they can seek settlement in a Baptist church. Once they have settled then they will be enrolled as a newly accredited minister.

There may, however, be people in your church who believe they are being called to some form of **lay-ministry** (i.e. non-ordained). Again, having discussed this with their minister, they should contact their regional minister who will explain the various options. All Baptist colleges now run courses suitable for preparing people to become lay-preachers and/or lay-pastors and your regional minister will explain how these can be accessed. Those people who complete such a course and have at least two years experience can apply to be a BUGB 'recognised' lay-pastor or lay-preacher. Further details on this are available from the BU Ministry department or your association. In addition, some associations have 'locally recognised' ministries and again, your regional minister will be able to explain if this is the case in your association.

6
Leadership
Deacons, Elders, Both or Neither

The vast majority of Baptist churches have deacons. However, some have elders as well as, or instead of, deacons. Others have a 'leadership team' which may or may not be sub-divided into deacons and elders. Some small churches have none of these and a few churches have developed a totally different leadership structure! The church secretary will, almost always, be a member of the diaconate or leadership team. Sometimes they are elected from that group to be the secretary and sometimes they will be an *ex-officio* member of the group following their appointment as secretary.

Fortunately it is not the role of this book to say which is the best way to do things! It is also not the role of this book to look in detail at the function and responsibility of leaders. There is, however, an excellent book written by Paul Beasley-Murray on this very subject. Subtitled 'A guide for elders and deacons in Baptist churches', *Radical Leaders,* which was updated in 2005 should, in my view, be read by everyone in leadership in our churches.

What I will do in this chapter is look at some of the practical and administrative issues of leadership.

More than one group of leaders?

In the introduction to the book mentioned above, Paul Beasley-Murray asks the question 'What's the difference between deacons and elders?' He then goes on to note that the usual distinction between the 'spiritual' (elders) and the 'practical' (deacons) cannot easily be maintained and gives a couple of examples to illustrate this. I would go further and say that everything that we do in church life has a spiritual and practical side to it.

37

This leads on to one of my two main concerns where churches have elders *and* deacons. This is the issue of where one group (deacons) is seen by the church as less important or less spiritual than the other (elders). This can be exacerbated if the minister chooses only (or mainly) to attend elders' meetings. From experience I know how demoralising this can become for the deacons. Whilst their roles will be different, both groups should consist of spiritual people with the gift of leadership. The Acts 6.1–6 passage, taken by many to be the appointment of the first deacons, clearly states that they were to be people who were 'full of the Holy Spirit and wisdom'. I would, therefore, encourage any church which has such a dual leadership structure to see their two groups as different but equal.

My other main concern is that there needs to be good communication between the two groups and there are a number of ways this can be facilitated. Ideally this will be through holding regular joint meetings. For example, Stockton Tabernacle has over 400 members and three ministers plus a children's worker and a youth worker. In addition to this five member ministerial team, their leadership team consists of nine deacons and ten elders. The whole team meets together bi-monthly to discuss major items with the elders and deacons having separate meetings in the other months. There will also be churches with much smaller numbers where elders regularly attend deacons meetings. If holding joint meetings isn't practicable then it is vital that someone briefs each group on what the other has been discussing!

Note that because of the great variety within our churches I will use the term 'leaders' for the rest of this chapter and leave you to interpret that for your situation.

Leaders are Trustees

It is an important aspect of our Baptist understanding of church that the final decision-making authority is the church meeting. However, under charity law, the group within the church who 'have the general control and management of the administration of the charity (church)' are regarded as the managing trustees. This is an important part of their role and consequently I have devoted the whole of a later chapter to this. In virtually every Baptist church this will be the diaconate (including the minister and elders where appointed) or the leadership team. As we move towards the time when all churches will have to register formally with the Charity Commission, churches will have to clearly identify in their trust deeds and constitution who the managing trustees are. The constitution will also need to include a clause that allows a minister, as a managing trustee, to be paid. The BUGB model constitution gives some suggested wording for these and help will be given to churches when the time for registration arrives. In addition the Faith and Unity Department of BUGB has produced a leaflet that reflects theologically on trusteeship which will help local church leaders understand the issues.

Appointing leaders

Your church's constitution will give the procedures for electing leaders and it is important that you, as church secretary, are fully aware of these. You will need to make sure that sufficient notice is given when nominations are due and that the correct procedures have been followed when nominations are made. You should also be aware of the majority needed for someone to be elected. In many churches this will be a simple majority, but in others it may be a two-thirds majority or even higher.

Sometimes when there are more candidates than vacancies a split vote can result in insufficient people achieving the required majority. This will mean that there are unnecessary vacancies on the leadership. There are ways round this! One is to have a second vote. If there are, for example, three vacancies and fewer than three nominees have achieved the required majority, then the names of the three who received the highest number of votes are put into a second ballot. All those who receive the required majority in the second vote are duly elected.

The second method is easier and is the one used in my own

church. It is also the one suggested by Paul Beasley-Murray in chapter 2 of *Radical Leaders*. In this case you allow members to have as many votes are there are candidates. So if there are five nominations for three vacancies, then members can vote for as many of those five as they believe God is calling to serve in this role. Providing they achieve the required majority then the three with the most votes are elected.

Leaders' meetings

There are a number of practical aspects to leaders' meetings which it is good to review regularly. Just because things have happened in the same way for the last ten years doesn't mean they have to continue in the same way for the next ten. Whilst I am not advocating change for change's sake, it does no harm for leaders to reflect whether their current practices need to be modified from time to time.

Frequency: most leaders will have a monthly business meeting – although others will meet more or less often. These meetings should, if possible, be supplemented by an occasional (or regular) prayer-breakfast, social evening or dayaway. Leadership is as much about relationships as about business so it is good to have opportunities to meet together without an agenda.

Venue: some leaders will always meet in a formal setting in church – possibly around a table. Others will always meet in someone's home where the chairs are more comfortable! Of course, larger churches with twenty people on their leadership may have difficulty in finding a home with enough room for them all. The venue, however, will affect the dynamics of the meeting so choose carefully.

Chairing the meeting: this is usually undertaken by the minister as part of his or her leadership role. However not all ministers make good 'chairs' and, in any case, there may well be times when it is seen to be more appropriate for another suitably-gifted leader to undertake this role. This can be on an occasional or more permanent basis.

Timing: it is a good idea to set a time limit on leaders' meetings that all are happy with. There will be times when circumstances necessitate over-running but this should be the exception rather than the rule.

Preparation: it is important that an agenda, or list of items to be discussed, is circulated in advance of the meeting. Where possible this should also include some brief explanation of each item – e.g. instead of just putting 'Alpha Course' on the agenda, put 'Alpha Course – we need to decide whether this is the right time to start a new course'. This will, in theory, enable people to come to the meeting having given some prayerful consideration to the items that will be discussed.

Minutes: it is helpful if the leaders can decide together when they would like to see the minutes (or 'action notes' as they are sometimes called) of their meeting. This should, of course, take into account the time restraints on the person responsible for producing them. Ideally, particularly if people need reminding what they have agreed to do, they should be produced and circulated as quickly as possible.

Leaders and the church meeting

Leaders are appointed to lead but they are also servants of the church and sometimes this can be a difficult balancing act. It is important to remember that the church meeting is the final decision-making authority and that the leaders should not make decisions that are not really theirs to make.

In practice the church meeting will normally delegate some decisions to the leaders. This level of delegation will vary considerably between churches and will, to some extent, depend on the size of the church with larger churches tending to delegate more than smaller ones. As church secretary you should keep an eye on this to avoid the two main problems that can occur. On one hand, a church meeting that delegates very little can end up spending a long time discussing trivialities. On the other, a church meeting can spend all its time simply rubber-stamping decisions that others have made. Neither of these two situations is good for the health of the church!

As leaders, however, the leadership has a responsibility to guide the church in the decisions it needs to make. In most instances this will mean giving a firm and clear lead by making recommendations that have been carefully thought through and, where possible, agreed unanimously. However, leaders should not take offence if their recommendation is not accepted. God does sometimes speak though ordinary church members as well.

As mentioned earlier, there is much more on the subject of church leadership in the book *Radical Leaders* published by BUGB. Other publications that might be helpful are the *'Help! I'm a ....' Guideline Leaflets* produced by the BUC. These cover the roles of church secretary (C19), Church Treasurer (C20), Deacon (C18) and Managing Trustee (C17). They are all available on the BUGB website.

Finally, you might want to reflect on what this cartoon says about the leadership of this church!

THE CHURCH KITCHEN

7
The Church

It really goes without saying that the church is not the building but the people; it is, however, good to be reminded occasionally that this is the case! In particular, Baptists understand that the church is a 'community of believers gathered by the Holy Spirit in the name of Jesus Christ for worship, witness and service.' (from the 'What makes a Baptist?' page on the BUGB website). This chapter will look at what happens when people join the church, how we can help them understand and fulfil their responsibilities as members, and some thoughts on what happens when people leave.

Joining the church

In today's post-modern culture, people are generally wary of joining anything! Consequently many churches will have a higher proportion of regular attenders in their congregation who are not members than would have been the case in the past. Baptists recognise, however, that the New Testament emphasises the value of committed relationships and that we are called to express and grow in our faith in a community of love. Consequently, Baptists have traditionally stressed the importance of becoming members alongside the importance of believers' baptism. For those churches wishing to explore the changing concepts of membership and belonging to a local church, the BUGB Faith and Unity Department have produced a pack on this subject as part of their 'Joined up Thinking' series.

Your church's constitution and rules may outline the procedures by which people become members but, generally speaking, people wishing to become members will speak to the minister or, possibly, the church secretary. Their names will then need to be taken to a church meeting to be voted on before they can become members.

The process in between will vary between churches but will usually involve bringing the name to the deacons who will appoint two of their number (or one deacon and one other church member) as visitors. The visitors will meet with the applicant and then bring a report to the church meeting. The purpose of the visit is to ensure that the applicant has made a personal Christian commitment, shares the beliefs of the church and understands the responsibilities of membership. The visit also provides opportunity for the applicant to learn more about the church.

Churches may not always follow this procedure if people are already in membership of another Baptist church and wanting to 'transfer' their membership. However, there are advantages in doing so anyway in that it gives an opportunity for the applicant to find out more about the church they are joining.

Once someone has been accepted into membership the usual procedure is for them to be welcomed in at the next convenient Communion Service. As church secretary, you need to make sure that this happens. The BUGB Book *Gathering for Worship* has suitable material for this.

Ideally and theologically, baptism and membership should go together for new Christians and it is always good when a baptismal service also includes the reception into membership of those who have just been baptised. If at all possible, the baptismal candidates should have some form of preparation course which will look at church membership as well as baptism. One useful book for this is *Baptism and Belonging* by Rob Warner (BUGB).

If you are a 'closed membership' church then only those people who have been baptised as believers may become members. Most closed membership churches will have some form of associate members list to which non-baptised people can be added. Many churches that have closed membership have this written into their foundation trust deed and, at the moment, there is no way to change this.

Some churches find it helpful to put together a membership pack for new members. This could contain such items as a welcome letter, the church constitution and rules, a membership list, a Gift Aid form and whatever else you feel to be appropriate.

The responsibilities of membership

Your church may have its own list of membership responsibilities but the one in the BUGB model constitution is given below as an example. As part of the joining process, new members should have been made aware of these, but the church leadership should also give some thought as to how people can be helped to fulfil them. Some questions you and the others in the leadership might like to think about are given in italics as part of this list.

The responsibilities of church membership include

- Attending worship and participating in church activities. *Does everyone know which activities take place when and where? Are there people who need help with transport or babysitting in order to help them attend? Is there a system in place for spotting when people stop coming on Sundays? Are there people who need some encouragement to become more involved? (And who is the right person to do this encouraging?)*

- Personal prayer and Bible study. *Does the church produce a prayer diary or provide prayer topics for members? Is there some mechanism for suggesting and/or providing Bible reading aids?*

- Helping the church whenever possible by using abilities to advance the purpose and vision of the church through its activities. This may mean working behind the scenes on administrative tasks and helping with practical projects. *How are the gifts of members identified? Are there ways of making sure that people are encouraged to use their gifts as appropriate? Have you got a copy of* Discovering the Gifts of Church Members *published by BUGB?*

- Attending and participating in regular church meetings. *Are there ways in which you can make church meetings something that more people actually want to come to? In larger churches in particular, has thought been given to ways in which everyone can be involved? Are there people who need help with transport or babysitting in order to help them attend? Do you hold your church meetings at times when most people are able to attend?*

◆ Giving regular financial support to the church in proportion to personal resources and circumstances. *Is there regular teaching on this subject? Does everyone know about giving under Gift Aid?*

Leaving the church

People leave the church for a number of reasons and in a variety of ways.

Some die and then there is an opportunity for farewells and thanksgiving to be expressed at a funeral or remembrance service.

Some people move away. It is helpful if the church has some sort of policy for saying goodbye and thank you to such people. This could include a farewell card signed by as many people as possible, a farewell lunch after a Sunday service and/or prayers in the service. (See the 'Blessing Departing Members' section in the BUGB book *Gathering for Worship*.) Care needs to be taken, however, that there is some consistency in practice so that the departure of the elderly, but quiet, faithful member who leaves to live nearer her family is not treated significantly differently than the departure of the former church secretary and his wife! Of course, this will depend on the church knowing in advance that someone is about to move. The people leaving may want someone to write to the Baptist church nearest to where they will be living asking them to make contact – but many will not, preferring to look for a new church themselves.

Some people stay in the area but move to a different church. Often they will do so without telling anyone until they have settled in a new church which makes it difficult to have any sort of formal goodbye. However a card might still be appropriate or maybe a letter from the church thanking them for their fellowship and participation in the life of the church in the past. A letter of commendation to their new church could also be sent. For some more thoughts on this subject, have a look at Training Notes TN27 in the resources section of John Truscott's website.

Some people simply stop attending any sort of church and numerous books and articles have been written on why this happens. Whatever the causes, however, happen it does and, as church secretary, you should ensure that the church regularly reviews its membership list to see if there are names that need to be removed from it. Hopefully this won't happen until the people concerned have been visited or, at the very least, contacted in some way. When such names are brought to a church meeting for deletion it does need to be handled very carefully as there is usually some emotional reaction to the proposal. Many churches have some sort of associate members list to which such people can be transferred so that contact can be maintained, at least for a time.

Maintaining records

As church secretary you will need to make sure that the members' roll is updated regularly with details of those joining the church. The names of those that leave, for whatever reason, will need to be deleted. This can be done in a special book or in a list maintained on the computer (See section on Data Protection in chapter 12).

It is also a good idea to keep a separate list of people who join or leave and the reason for this – joining following baptism, personal testimony or by transfer; leaving because of death, transfer, resignation or deletion. This will help considerably when completing the BUGB annual return form (see section on annual returns in chapter 12). Keeping a record of the number of people becoming Christians or being baptised during the year will also help with this.

If you are in an LEP (Local Ecumenical Partnership), then you will need to make sure that denominational lists are maintained alongside the common roll. This can be as simple as noting a letter by each person's name on the common roll (B for Baptist, M for Methodist etc) – some people may have more than one letter if they have been jointly initiated, or officially 'extended' their membership. You may need to keep other records to help with the completion of the return forms of the other denominations. This might include things like infant/believers' baptisms, confirmations and funerals taking place in the church. Further information on what is required can be obtained from the national offices of the partner denominations.

Many churches will produce some form of directory or contact list of members for circulation amongst the fellowship. You should really check that individuals are happy for their phone number and/or e-mail address to be included on such a list. There is also potential danger in including children on such lists if there is the possibility of people outside the fellowship having access to the list.

8
Sunday Services

Like much else in Baptist life there is great diversity within our worship services, particularly in terms of music – organs, music-groups, choirs, traditional hymns and new songs can all be found in Baptist churches – and some will have all of these at one time or another. But, despite the differences that exist, there will always be certain organisational aspects that you as church secretary need to be aware of.

Preparing the building

Whether you have your own building or you meet in a school or community centre, there will always be some work needing to be done in order to prepare the building for services. At the most basic this will simply mean ensuring that the church is opened up in good time, the heating is on and the place is clean and tidy. For some, however, much more will need to be done including the setting up of all the chairs, the sound system, screen and data-projector.

The wise church secretary will not do all this themselves although, particularly in smaller churches, they may feel there is no alternative. However, most churches do operate some sort of rota system for all that needs to be done and where this can be done it should be. One of the first things I did when I became a church secretary in 1984 was to introduce a 'duty deacon' rota to make sure that I didn't have to open up every week as my predecessors had done.

Welcoming people

All churches, whatever their size, need to have people situated near the entrance to welcome people as they arrive for worship. Again this will probably be done on a rota basis. These people should be friendly and welcoming to all regardless of age, gender, colour, ability or anything else. It is good if they can welcome regulars (including children) by name but it is not good if they spend their time catching up on the latest news from their friends and block up the entrance! Remember, first impressions are important and these door stewards or welcome team members will be the first people that visitors meet.

It is also a good idea to have a separate group of people as a 'newcomers' team' who have a specific role of looking out for visitors and newcomers and helping them to feel at ease. For some really helpful advice on setting up a newcomers' team, visit John Truscott's website and download TN14 from his Training Notes page. You can print up to thirty copies of any of John's resource papers for use within your church free of charge.

Another useful resource can be found on the 'Through the Roof' website. This gives guidelines for welcoming people with disabilities. Go to www.throughtheroof.org and click on 'Roofbreaker' guides.

Visiting preachers

At one time or another most churches make use of visiting preachers – people who come to lead worship and/or preach at Sunday services. For some churches without a minister and with few in the congregation with the time and gifts to lead services, this is a way of life. For others it will just be an occasional event. Whilst the comments below may seem obvious to some of you, hopefully others will pick up some helpful advice. Some churches will have a 'pulpit supply secretary', or similar, who will take care of all of this. In others it will be the responsibility of the church secretary.

The first contact with the visitor should be to establish date and time and whether they are expected to lead the whole service or just preach. If you expect your visitor to fit in with a sermon series or lectionary this needs to be made clear at this stage. Other useful details to mention are …

◆ whether the service will include communion or not

◆ details of hymn-books used (if any)

◆ whether children will be present and for how long and, if so, is a 'children's talk' expected

◆ the usual length of the service

and when you will next be in touch with them.

The second contact will be to check that everything is OK and to receive details of the songs they wish to use (if relevant). You may also need to check that they know how to find the church and, if appropriate, explain the parking arrangements. Other details may need to be mentioned – for example, if one of your deacons always leads in prayer at a communion service, it is helpful if the visitor knows this in advance.

On the day, they will need to be welcomed and helped to feel at ease. Even the most experienced lay-preacher or minister will have some slight nervousness when visiting a church for the first time. Make sure that microphones are explained and ask them if there is anything they need to know beforehand. Arrangements for offerings and communion can vary greatly so it may help if some brief explanation of the norm for your church is given.

After the service the secretary should make sure that the visitor is paid. But how much? This is never an easy question to answer and must always be at the discretion of the local church. One thing that should never happen is for the visitor to be asked how much they are owed.

The website for the West of England Baptist Association has the following advice and is reproduced with their permission.

> We all recognise that 'the labourer is worthy of his hire' but there are times when any sort of recognition of remuneration for the hours of preparation and the time spent in worship leading seems to point to an enormous figure. Many preachers will spend at least five or six hours preparing for each service, some many more plus the service time, travel time and expenses on the day. Therefore it would not be unreasonable for an average sized church (seventy members) to offer a fee of forty pounds (£40) per service. Larger churches can no doubt

NOTHING SPIRITUAL ABOUT CHAOS

afford more. Travel and significant administrative costs should be met in full over and above the fee. Where public transport or taxis have to be used those costs are easy to ascertain. Where a preacher's own vehicle is used, a rate of 20p per mile, which is the rate paid by the Baptist Union for those who attend committee meetings, would seem to be reasonable.

Whatever sum you do agree to pay should be reviewed regularly.

Communion services

'The secretary should regard himself as primarily responsible for the arrangements of the communion service, even though one or two women members prepare the bread and wine, and set the table. He will advise the deacons where they are to sit and will advise those who are to serve or to pray.' So wrote Richard Fairbairn and Ronald Thomson in their 1965 *Church Secretary's Handbook* and I have often used this passage as an example of how things have moved on in forty years. Certainly in my own church both women and men take their turn in preparing the table for communion. We also have more informal arrangements for which deacons will serve and deacons only pray if invited to do so by the minister. Others of you may have rotas for who will serve or lead in prayer but I doubt if there are many churches which have all the deacons sitting at the front during communion! However it is still true to say that someone (usually the church secretary) should oversee the practicalities of communion.

A spare sermon?

At least one former church secretary I know of always kept a spare sermon in the vestry in case the minister or visiting preacher didn't turn up. You might not want to go that far, but you might like to give some thought as to what you would do in that situation. Emergencies do happen and ministers (or members of their family) have had to be rushed into hospital on a Sunday although, fortunately, this is a rare occurrence!

Dedications and baptisms

Sometimes a Sunday service will include one of these and the likelihood is that there will be more visitors than on a normal Sunday. This may mean that extra welcomers or stewards will be needed.

For services that include **infant presentation and dedication**, there will not be too much additional organisation required, although reserved seats for the family and close friends would be helpful. The minister will have met with the family beforehand to discuss the details of the service. In the absence of a minister you may find yourself involved in this. The BUGB *Gathering for Worship* book has some useful background material as well as two suggested service patterns. If your church has a cradle roll secretary or someone else who keeps details of the children who have been brought for dedication, then they will need to be kept informed. Some churches give certificates to the parents and BUGB produce some for this very purpose. You will need to make sure that these are obtained and filled in before the service.

Baptismal services require greater organisation as there is usually a pool to be filled and heated and changing rooms to be organised. Churches may find it helpful to appoint a baptismal co-ordinator who will make sure the above things are done and that the candidates are happy with the practical arrangements. They may also take responsibility for obtaining and filling in the baptismal certificate and for informing the *Baptist Times* of the baptism. Again, *Gathering for Worship* has useful material for baptismal services. Of course a baptismal service doesn't have to take place in a church and they have been known to take place in swimming pools, rivers and the sea. If you have a portable baptismal pool then you could have an open-air baptismal service in your car park or anywhere you like – providing you have some way of filling it!

9
Weddings and Funerals

By their very nature, weddings will normally be planned well in advance but you may only have a few days' notice for a funeral. However, they will both be occasions when many visitors will be in your building so it is doubly important to make sure it is warm, clean, tidy and welcoming. You will also need to make sure that the building is opened up in good time – visitors often arrive earlier than 'normal' church people – and that someone will be around at the end to lock up. (Don't rely on the minister to do this after a funeral as s/he may well be going on to the crematorium or cemetery.) Of course if the church has a caretaker then this will usually be his or her role.

Funerals will normally be organised by the minister in consultation with the family. If you don't have a minister then you may find it helpful to have good relationships with ministers in the locality who will be willing to lead funerals for you. Of course, it doesn't have to be a minister who leads the service, but if you find yourself in the position of being asked to take a funeral you may find it helpful to get some advice from a local minister. The BUGB book *Gathering for Worship* has a number of service patterns for a variety of situations and circumstances.

If you want to know more about what needs to be done following a death then visit www.dwp.gov.uk/resourcecentre/social_fund. asp and download leaflet D49 *What to do after a death in England and Wales* (or D49S if you live in Scotland).

If your church is often used for funerals then, during an interregnum, it is worth getting in touch with the local undertaker(s) to let them know who to contact whilst there is no minister in post.

Weddings are a bit more complicated. At the time of writing marriages may be celebrated in a church only if it is registered for marriages. If your church is registered then an authorised person (appointed by the church) or a local registrar must be present to witness and register the marriage. Information about this and an application form to register the building are on the website www.gro.gov.uk/gro/content/marriages/

Anyone can be an authorised person and churches can appoint more than one if they so choose. Whilst many ministers are authorised persons, they generally have enough to do in conducting a wedding without worrying about the registration side. Full information about the duties of an authorised person are provided on appointment. You will also be able to obtain details from your local register office. This can be found via the local phone book or on www.gro.gov.uk . The latter way will also provide you with a link to your local register office's web-page which may have some helpful information about weddings.

Once again, *Gathering for Worship* will come in useful if you are asked to lead a service of marriage. As well as two main service patterns, there are also some helpful legal and pastoral notes. There have been plans to change the law in relation to marriages but, at the time of writing, these have been shelved.

In addition to providing the building and the minister, some churches are able to offer other services to the 'happy couple' – sometimes these can be provided free of charge or at cost price. With the cost of an average wedding at around £12,000 at the time of writing, a church that is able to help in this way will be appreciated by many! Depending on resources, facilities and suitable people, such a wedding package could include cars, flowers, printed orders of service, reception venue and catering, cake, photographer, musicians and a video. (Note that wedding videos that include music – live or pre-recorded – need a licence to comply with copyright law. For more information go to www.videolicence.co.uk)

Most churches will also want to run some form of marriage preparation classes and there is a variety of material available for this, including *Happy Ever After?* by Paul Beasley-Murray (BUGB) and *The Marriage Preparation Course* by Nicki and Sila Lee from Holy Trinity, Brompton – the home of the Alpha Course. For more information on this visit www.themarriagecourse.org

10

The Wider Baptist Family

Whilst Baptist churches are autonomous they should not be isolationist! From the very earliest days Baptist churches have grouped themselves together in associations and Unions. Today most Baptist churches in England and Wales belong to the Baptist Union of Great Britain and/or one of the regional associations. Most belong to both. Some churches in Wales belong to the Baptist Union of Wales as well as, or instead of, BUGB.

Some Baptist churches are in Local Ecumenical Partnerships which will also need to relate to the regional and national groups of their partner denominations. If this includes you then you need to make sure you know who is your county ecumenical officer or the secretary of your sponsoring body. You will need to liaise with them over the support arrangements for your LEP, and when it is time for your review.

Regional associations

'Baptist churches have always linked together in regional associations to support one another in their task of reaching out with the Good News of Jesus' (BUGB website).

The main aims of the associations are to encourage, equip and resource their member churches in their work and mission, although they will do this in a variety of ways. Each of the associations has regional ministers who will work with ministers and churches through the good times and not-so-good times. They can help in times of crisis and when churches are looking for new ways to move forward. They can provide pastoral support and mission advice. At least one regional minister will work with churches looking for a new minister and with ministers looking for a new church.

(See chapter 5 for more on this subject.) Associations will also have people who can help churches with financial or administrative queries. Some of these are paid staff, others are volunteers.

Associations will all have different structures and ways of organising themselves but, in the end, they are all there to help their member churches so please use them! If your church is in membership of an association then you will receive regular communications from them in the post, by e-mail or both. You will also have a directory or yearbook which gives details of the staff and the committees as well as listing the member churches. If your church is not in membership of an association then you can find the contact details for the region in which your church is situated by visiting the associations' page on the BU website or by ringing Baptist House. Whilst the associations have a similar role to BUGB (see below) their key strength is that they are regional and will have greater local knowledge. If you have a query about anything to do with church life try your association first. If they are unable to help they should be able to point you towards someone who can.

In order to be effective, associations rely on ministers and church secretaries to pass on the information sent to others in their church. Most associations run regular training events on a whole range of subjects such as preaching, child-protection, youth work, church finance, music and worship – but they need *you* to let the people in your church know about them! In addition, all associations will hold Assemblies or association days which include some business. It is important that as many member churches as possible are represented at these. As church secretary you may well find these events helpful in that they are a very good way of meeting people from other local Baptist churches – including other church secretaries.

Associations also need to be kept up-to-date with changes in your church – new minister, secretary or treasurer as well as changes of address, phone number or e-mail. The best way to do this is through your association administrator, secretary or equivalent person. Their contact details are on the BUGB web-page referred to above.

BUGB

The Baptist Union of Great Britain is a union of churches, associations and colleges and has its resource base in Baptist House in Didcot, Oxfordshire. For contact details see the resources chapter at the end of this book. The staff who work there do so in order to support the work and mission of the member churches, associations and colleges. Currently the work is done within six departments and each department has its own page on the BUGB website where more information is available. Below is a brief summary of the work of each department which should give you some idea of the range of guidance and support offered to churches.

The **Finance and Administration Department** spends a lot of its time, according to the current head of department, 'doing things that churches don't want to do so that they can spend their time on their real work'. In other words they keep up-to-date with all the various legislation and regulations and then assist churches through advice and training. One key resource produced by this department is the series of BUC *Guideline* leaflets which are extremely helpful. They can be downloaded from the website or ordered from the BUC office at Baptist House. They are regularly updated to take account of changes in legislation and new ones are added as appropriate. Churches are also kept up-to-date with financial and legal issues through **Transform** which is sent to ministers and church secretaries three times a year. (Note that church secretaries are sent two copies, one of which is intended for the church treasurer.) This department is also responsible for Home Mission grants, trust work, running the two Baptist pension schemes and maintaining the Union's database – among other things! It is important to note that churches should contact this department (or their association) on legal, tax or property matters. This is because these are areas where specialist knowledge of Baptist churches is quite important.

With only two members of staff, the **Faith and Unity Department** is the smallest of the Union's departments but it does have responsibility for a number of important areas of work. It has three key tasks. The first is to nurture relationships with Christians both in this country and throughout the world. One way this is done is by supporting and resourcing member churches which are in Local Ecumenical Partnerships. The department's second key task is to reflect on issues of faith and doctrine, and deepen our shared life of prayer and worship. This includes providing monthly prayers of intercession on the website and producing material to help churches think through theological issues. The third key task is to promote campaigning and action on issues of social justice and up-to-date details of the work they do in this area can be found in **Trans*form*** or through the regular e-mails sent from the department.

The **Ministry Department** is responsible for developing and maintaining support systems for ministers in training, in pastoral charge and in specialist ministry. As part of that it oversees the accreditation process and the work of the National Settlement Team. There is also a member of staff dealing with child-protection issues.

The **Department for Research and Training in Mission** doesn't itself do mission but is there to enable and resource churches to do mission. The department has a number of mission advisers and a racial justice co-ordinator. All the advisers can help with any area of mission but they also have their specialities – such as urban mission, social inclusion, youth work, evangelism and church planting. The department also administers 'Green Shoots' and 'Against the Stream' grants for mission projects.

The **Communications Department** was set up in September 2005 and its main aim is to ensure that the mission and purposes of BUGB are communicated effectively. This is done through printed media, videos and DVDs, the website and events such as the Baptist Assembly. They can also help churches in their contact with the media both in times of crisis and in developing ongoing relationships.

The final department is the **General Secretariat** which currently consists of the General Secretary, the General Manager and their two PAs. Their role is to provide leadership within the Union, facilitate strategic initiatives at national level and encourage co-operation between BUGB members. They also, along with the BUGB President, represent the Union at national and international gatherings.

I could finish this section by providing you with information about the work of the BU Council and its committees – but I won't! Details are on the website if you are interested. However, just as associations rely on church secretaries in particular to pass on information to their churches, so does the Baptist Union. As well as **Transform**, you will, if you are in membership of BUGB, receive details of the Baptist Assembly, Leading Edge (the Baptist holiday event) and other national events. Your church will be invited to appoint delegates to the Assembly and will also have a vote in the vice-presidential election each year. One vital document that you will receive every year if you are in membership with BUGB or an association is the BU annual return form – and I will look at this in more detail in chapter 12.

Note also that the Baptist Unions of Scotland and Wales will carry out similar work for their churches although on a smaller scale. Their contact details are included in chapter 15.

Financial help available

Grants and loans are both available from the Baptist Union for churches needing financial help with their buildings or with mission. In addition many associations will have loan funds and some may also be able to give small grants. Some associations will also run a 'church of the year' or 'church project' scheme whereby one or two churches each year are chosen to receive specific help from others in the association.

Each year over £1.5m is given to churches and other ministries in the form of Home Mission grants. These are national grants administered locally. Any church wishing to explore the possibility of receiving a Home Mission grant to help towards the cost of ministry should contact their regional minister who will be able to explain the process.

One per cent of the money given to Home Mission (see chapter 14) each year is allocated to the 'Against the Stream' fund which gives one-off grants to churches involved in projects that alleviate poverty or the effects of poverty in the local community. The same amount of money is allocated to the 'Green Shoots' fund which gives grants to churches involved in innovative and imaginative evangelistic initiatives. For more information about either of these, contact the BUGB Mission Department or the mission specialist in your association.

For details of loans and, in some special cases, grants for building work contact your association or the BUGB finance office. There is also the independent Baptist Building Fund which makes interest-free loans for the building, repair or extension of Baptist churches. Their contact details can be obtained from your association or BUGB

The international family

For the sake of completeness we shouldn't forget that Baptists exist in other countries as well. 'Baptists see themselves as part of the world church with a mission, through the gospel, to bring people everywhere into God's family. Baptists live and work in every corner of the globe and various regional associations exist to help them in their mission. The Baptist Union of Great Britain is one of the founder members of the European Baptist Federation (www.ebf.org) and the Baptist World Alliance (www.bwanet.org) which represents nearly 150,000 churches and more than forty million members' (BUGB website). Most churches will not have any direct link with these organisations but, through BUGB, we are part of the worldwide Baptist family.

BMS World Mission

Another way in which we are part of a much larger family is through the work of BMS World Mission which all Baptist churches are encouraged to support. Currently they are working in around forty countries on four continents in the areas of church planting, development, disaster relief, education, health, media and advocacy. 'BMS believes in holistic mission, an approach that stays true to the Christian call to evangelisation without neglecting the duty to take care of the physical needs of the poor. BMS works through long, medium and short term workers, teams and volunteers, as well as a large number of supported national workers around the world, providing people, funding, training and expertise in the core areas of our work.' (From www.bmsworldmission.org)

Churches are encouraged to appoint a BMS World Mission representative who will receive information from BMS and then pass it on in appropriate ways to their church. BMS World Mission also has a number of regional co-ordinators who are always willing to visit churches in their area to educate and inspire them about world mission. For details of your regional co-ordinator contact BMS World Mission which is also based in Baptist House.

Other Baptist organisations

And finally in this section are details of some of the various Baptist organisations that exist which may be of use to you or others in your church. The full list is included in the *BU Directory* which is produced annually. Where there are websites these are included. Contact details for other organisations can be obtained from your association or BUGB.

Campers and Caravanners may be interested in the **Guild of Baptist Campers** (www.baptistcampers.org.uk) or the **Baptist Caravan Fellowship** (www.thebcf.org.uk), both of which organise regular camps or rallies around the country.

The **Baptist Holiday Fellowship** (www.baptistholidayfellowship.co.uk) has self-catering apartments in Minehead and also organises tours to Europe and the Holy Land.

The **Baptist Peace Fellowship** (www.baptist-peace.org.uk) aims to provide a fellowship for Baptists who find that the use of military force cannot be reconciled with the teaching of Jesus

Christ and his acceptance of the Cross.

The **Baptist Union Retreat Group** organises retreats and encourages the life of 'prayer and silence' and the training of retreat leaders

BUild (Baptist Union initiative with people with learning disabilities) provides speakers, discipleship and educational materials and conferences for all in Baptist churches who are working with people with learning disabilities.

The **Retired Baptist Ministers' Housing Society** provides accommodation for retired Baptist ministers and their spouses. Some ministers can get very anxious about where they will live when they retire. If this is the case with your minister, point them in the direction of this organisation.

11
Managing Trustees

Introduction

The managing (or charity) trustees of a charity are defined as the group of people who actually have the general control and management of the administration of the charity. Charities usually have a board of trustees, directors, or management committee who take key strategic decisions about the activities of their organisation and ensure that the charity is well run.

Churches are charities – even if most aren't registered with the Charity Commission. In most Baptist churches it is the diaconate (including the minister) who, notwithstanding the role of the church meeting, 'have the general control and management of the administration of the charity'. As noted in chapter 7, some churches have elders as well as, or instead of, deacons and others have a leadership team, but titles aren't important. For the purposes of charity law the group in your church who are identified as 'leaders' are the managing trustees and in virtually every Baptist church this group will include the church secretary.

This might sound scary but it has actually always been the case and, for most churches, will just be about doing what you've been doing anyway. Most of it is just common sense (and quite Biblical too).

The Baptist Union Corporation has produced a number of very helpful *Guideline* leaflets which relate to the issue of trusteeship and they will be referred to in this chapter. They are all available from the BUGB website . This chapter is based on Leaflet C17: *Help! I'm a Managing Trustee.*

Churches, the law and the Charity Commission

Charitable status brings significant benefits in the form of Gift Aid and other allowances. Therefore the proper administration of charity funds is very important because of the need to follow good practices and meet the requirements of charity law generally and the Charities Act 1993 in particular.

Of course, the need to ensure that the financial aspects of church life are well organised is not just related to legal responsibilities. Our Christian faith should make us want to ensure that there can be no doubt that all aspects of the administration of the church are handled carefully, effectively and with absolute integrity.

The Charity Commission is a legally established body that has particular responsibility for all charities, including churches. They have legal powers to ensure that charities are well run and there are good reasons for this. It is undesirable for the public to give money to a good cause and then for it to be misused as this has an adverse effect on all charities. The Charity Commission can, therefore, use its legal powers to intervene where there is evidence of irregularities. They also offer guidance and encourage good practice so that charity resources are used well.

The Charity Commission has a website www.charity-commission. gov.uk and this provides information about charities and how managing trustees should operate. There are several publications that can be ordered from them or downloaded from the website. The three most useful ones are

CC3   *The Essential Trustee: What you need to know*

CC3a   *Responsibilities of a Charity Trustee (Summary).* Note that this is a summary of an earlier version of CC3 so may disappear at some point.

CC60   *Hallmarks of an Effective Charity*

Charity registration

Churches are charities because of their activities. The advancement of religion has been recognised as one of the objectives that makes an organisation or activity charitable. As I mentioned earlier, most churches are not registered with the Charity Commission. This is because they are currently excepted from registration. Most other charities are registered, so this can cause confusion.

Churches do not normally have a charity number and this can cause problems when filling in forms that assume all charities have a number! Don't be tempted to use the charity number of your local association – you just need to write in that as a church you are a charity 'excepted from registration'. The relevant *Guideline* leaflet (see next paragraph) explains this in more detail. If you have problems in this area (e.g. with a bank) you may find it helpful to show or send them a copy of that leaflet with the relevant sections highlighted.

The 'excepting regulations' will be changed – eventually – and churches will have to register. The application process will probably be selective, and may start with the largest churches in 2007. Don't worry though – BUGB will advise all member churches on what they will need to do when the time comes. For more information on this and how your church might like to prepare for registration, see Leaflet C16: *Churches and Charity Registration.*

Restrictions on who can become a Managing Trustee

A local church will have rules about selecting leaders, but anyone asked to serve will become a managing trustee. Consequently there are certain restrictions that a church needs to be aware of when appointing its leadership. A person cannot serve as a managing trustee if they ...

- ◆ are under eighteen years of age.
- ◆ have been convicted of an offence involving deception or dishonesty, unless the conviction is spent.
- ◆ are an un-discharged bankrupt or insolvent.
- ◆ have been convicted of a serious offence involving children.
- ◆ have previously been removed from trusteeship of a charity by the Court or the Charity Commissioners for misconduct or mismanagement.
- ◆ have been disqualified from being a company director.

In special circumstances the Charity Commissioners can waive these requirements but each case will be considered on its merits. By definition the granting of a waiver of the standard requirements will be exceptional.

In addition, managing trustees are not normally entitled to receive any financial benefit because of their role (other than reimbursement of reasonable and necessary out-of-pocket expenses). In other words, neither they nor close members of their family can normally be employed by the charity of which they are a trustee.

The Charity Commission accepts (at present) that these restrictions do not prevent the **minister** of a Baptist church from receiving a stipend whilst being a managing trustee. However, a paid administrator or youth worker, for example, can't be a deacon without obtaining specific permission from the Charity Commission.

Conflict with the Bible?

Some people will say ask why we have to follow the Charity Commission's rules when we should be following Biblical principles. But … the priorities set by the Charity Commission for a well-run charity do not need to conflict with the objectives and practices of a Baptist church … or the Bible!

The Charity Commission says that an effective charity will be clear about its objects, vision, mission and values and how it will achieve them. In church terms, this means that a church needs to be able to define its purpose and the plans it has for achieving that purpose. According to Ephesians 4.11–13, church leaders are there to prepare God's people for service and to build up the body of Christ. In other words, the role of the leaders is to help achieve the purpose of the church.

The Charity Commission says that the structure, policies and procedures of an effective charity enable it to achieve its mission and aims and deliver its services efficiently. In other words, our church structures should be there to enable the church to fulfil its mission. Acts 6.1–7 is a good example of the early church reorganising itself to enable its purposes to be achieved more effectively.

The Charity Commission says that an effective charity is run by a clearly identifiable trustee body that has the right balance of skills and experience to run the charity effectively and acts in the best interests of the charity. In church terms we need to make sure that those appointed as leaders have the necessary gifts and skills to fulfil their role and should, at all times, act in the best interest of the church. This should be the case anyway, regardless of what the Charity Commission says! 1 Peter 5.2–3 reminds us that church leaders are called to look after those in their care and to be 'examples to the flock'.

The Charity Commission says that an effective charity manages and uses its resources so as to optimise its potential. In a church context, this is all about making good use of the gifts and resources that God has given us to benefit the whole church. 1 Peter 4.10 is just one of a number of passages that encourage us to use the gifts God has given us to further his work.

The Charity Commission says that an effective charity is accountable to the public and other stakeholders in a way that is transparent and understandable. Honesty, integrity and openness should be part of our life together as Christians and Titus 2.7–8 is one passage that encourages this.

The Charity Commission says that an effective charity is flexible enough to influence and adapt to changes in the environment in which it works in order to meet the changing needs of those who use its services. As church leaders we need to be constantly looking to understand God's will for a particular situation and to look for new ways of advancing the kingdom 'making the most of every opportunity' – Ephesians 5.16.

The work of managing trustees

The main task of a managing trustee is to ensure that the charity is well run. Therefore, a good trustee will always act with integrity, in the best interests of the charity and without regard to their own interests. Hopefully this is what all leaders in the church will be seeking to do anyway.

A good trustee will ensure that:

- there is good management – particularly in the area of finance.
- there is mutual accountability and joint responsibility – it's all about working together and sharing the decisions.
- the charity (and its assets) are managed in accordance with the governing document – i.e. your church's constitution and trust deeds.
- the work of the charity is advanced. Churches should be about mission and not maintenance anyway!

A trustee must not take advantage of his or her position to make a financial gain, so conflicts of interest should be avoided – or properly managed. Legitimate expenses can be paid, but, as I said earlier, managing trustees cannot normally be employed by the charity they serve, neither can close relatives.

These rules are for the protection of the charity, and to ensure that it is quite clear to all that the individuals involved are not benefiting personally from charity funds.

This is an area where there is a little more flexibility than had previously been the case. Under certain conditions the Charity Commission will allow employment of, or the supply of goods to, a charity by a trustee or close relative without the need for the trustee to resign. For example, if a deacon has a printing company he may now (with permission) be able to do work for the church and provide printed publicity material. Be careful though – this is a privilege that comes on strict conditions. The proper processes must be observed in each case and the overriding principle is one of absolute integrity and accountability. It is important to be able to demonstrate that a payment to a trustee is in the best interests of the charity and that other options have been considered.

For more information visit the Charity Commission website.

Church finances

Even though your church will have a treasurer and, possibly, a book-keeper or finance group, all the managing trustees are responsible for overseeing the finances of the charity. This does not mean that everyone will have the same depth of understanding of the details but all trustees are jointly responsible for:

- ◆ **Budgets** – preparing and agreeing a budget and agreeing a reserves policy; the trustees should also regularly review the budget against actual income and expenditure, making adjustments if the income is too low or the expenditure too high!

- ◆ **Accounts** – ensuring that proper accounts records are maintained, and that at the end of the financial year the formal accounts are prepared and audited or examined as necessary.

- ◆ **Good management** – ensuring that the financial resources are spent on the purposes of the charity and preventing expenditure that is outside the declared objects of the charity. This also means making sure that bills and expense claims are paid promptly, and that any salaries are paid properly. Good management does not mean keeping all the money for a 'rainy day'. Sadly, churches and charities sometimes close with money in the bank that nobody has invested in legitimate activities. Trustees should positively seek good ways to spend money on achieving the church's declared objectives.

DO work together as a whole trustee body. Finances are a joint responsibility – facilitated by the treasurer but not his/her sole responsibility. Treasurers needs the support and help of all the leaders.

DO decide whose signatures will be used on cheques. At least two signatures are needed on cheques – always. **Never** sign a blank cheque. If you are signing a church cheque you **must** know what the cheque is for and to whom it is payable. Many charities (including churches) have lost money because this basic safeguard was ignored. It's not about distrusting the treasurer – it's about acting in the best interests of the church – and actually in the best interests of the treasurer as it protects him or her against accusations of fraud.

DO make financial reporting a regular feature of your meetings and ask questions of the treasurer if there are things you don't understand. You should also agree together what can be spent, on whose authority without referring back to the whole group. Some church meetings decide on a framework for spending – allowing leaders to spend on general items and emergency items up to an agreed sum without further reference to the members meeting. Other churches will authorise the leaders to spend in line with the agreed budget. You need to know the arrangements that apply to your church.

DON'T ignore warning signs. Sadly, even in church life, there are little problems that can turn into bigger problems because they are ignored. So, if the accounts are never ready for auditing, or if the auditor highlights a concern – it is the responsibility of all the trustees to follow this up

And whilst on the subject of finances, you might like to know that all church treasurers are encouraged to join ACAT (The Association of Church Accountants and Treasurers). Members receive a very comprehensive handbook and regular updates on financial issues. For details on how to join visit their website www.acat.uk.com or contact the BUGB finance office.

In addition the BUGB finance office has produced some helpful financial guideline leaflets including:

F5: *Taxation Guidance for churches and ministers*

F6: *Accounting Guidelines (for churches with a gross income of less that £100,000)*

F7: *Charity Accounts over £100,000*

F8: *Gift Aid Guidelines*

F9: *Charity Reserves*

Rules and regulations – don't worry!

Rules and regulations can seem overwhelming and many churches are concerned about the heavy responsibilities placed on them. Fortunately, Baptist churches can find help within the excellent set of *Guideline* leaflets produced by the Baptist

Union Corporation and regularly updated. These include the following:

C7:   *Health and Safety and fire precautions*

C9:   *Food safety*

C12: *Employment*

C13: *Disability Discrimination*

C14: *Data Protection*

And don't forget the importance of having a child protection policy. All these topics are also covered, albeit briefly, in the next chapter.

Buildings and property

Make sure you know who your property or 'holding' trustees are and contact them when contemplating purchase or sale of property, alterations, or major repairs. Most Baptist churches will have either the BUC or their regional Baptist Trust Company as their holding trustees. Note that contact with your trustees should be made as early as possible in the process and certainly before any work starts! Not only do they need to know what you are doing (and in many cases will have to give their permission) but they may have some useful observations to make and/or be able to put you in touch with other churches who have undertaken similar projects.

The BUC *Guideline* leaflets cover many issues relating to church property including the following:

A2:   *Buying a Manse*

A3:   *Selling a Manse*

A4:   *Shared ownership of a Manse*

A5:   *Letting a Manse*

A8:   *Leasing a property (owned in whole or part by a minister) to a church for use as a manse. (Formerly known as a 'Leaseback')*

B1:   *Church Trusts, Model Trusts and Property Trustees*

B2:   *Buying Land or Premises for a Church*

B3:   *Selling Church Land or Premises*

B4:   *Redeveloping Church Premises*

B5:   *Letting Church Premises*

B11:   *Churches and Leases*

C1:   *Burial Grounds*

C2:   *Church Closure*

C4:   *Church Amalgamation*

Decisions about property are very important ones that will need the decision of a church members' meeting – and often a 'special' meeting is required. Check your constitution!

If your church is a listed building, then all alterations will need the consent of the Listed Buildings Advisory Committee – provided it is in membership of BUGB or BUW and in trust with a Baptist Trust Corporation. Other Baptist churches with listed buildings will need to apply to their local planning authority for consent to make alterations.

More details are available in the following leaflets:

LB1:   *Introducing the Listed Buildings Advisory Committee*

LB2:   *Applying to the Listed Buildings Advisory Committee*

LB3:   *Advising Churches on Applications to the Listed Buildings Advisory Committee*

LB5:   *Looking After your Church Buildings*

LB6:   *Listed Buildings Application Form*

LB7:   *Furnishings in Listed Churches*

Please note that breach of listed building control is a criminal offence and the managing trustees could face prosecution!

Personal liability

This is an area which does worry some people. However it's not really an issue for sensible managing trustees – especially if you are careful in your activities and seek advice when you are in doubt about a decision. However, mistakes do happen – so if something does go wrong, don't just ignore it, take steps to put it right.

To avoid serious problems you need to make sure that you, as managing trustees …

- ◆ ensure that the church spends only what it can afford.
- ◆ maintain proper insurances – comprehensive, adequate and relevant to the church's activities.
- ◆ act sensibly.
- ◆ involve professional advisors where necessary.
- ◆ seek and accept advice.

If something has gone wrong and the managing trustees do not know how to proceed they **must** ask for help. Your first port of call should be the staff of the local association or your holding trustees (BUC or your regional Trust Company). If the problems relate to finance then you should contact the BUGB finance office.

If none of these people can help then the Charity Commission can help a charity that is in trouble and they may be able to work with you to overcome the problem.

10
All the Other Things that Need to be Done!

This chapter is where I have put all the things that didn't really fit elsewhere – or where I wanted to expand slightly on topics referred to briefly earlier on.

Annual returns

◆ Towards the end of November every church in membership of BUGB and/or a regional association will receive an annual return form. They are sent out through the associations and, normally, have to be returned via the association. Those churches not in membership of an association will have their forms sent out direct from Baptist House.

◆ There are a number of reasons for these forms – they enable the BUGB database to be kept up-to-date and to provide the relevant information for the BUGB *Directory*. They enable trends to be monitored (e.g. the number of children connected with our churches or the numbers of baptisms) and important research to be undertaken. Each year one particular aspect of church life (e.g. finance or mission) is featured on the form with churches being asked to respond to a number of questions on that subject.

◆ It is the responsibility of the church secretary – to whom the form is sent – to make sure they are returned as directed by the closing date (usually 31 January) even though others (e.g. the treasurer or minister) may well complete all or part of the forms.

◆ In addition, some associations may have their own forms although these may be sent out at a different time of year.

◆ For churches that are part of a Local Ecumenical Partnership there will also be forms from the other partner denominations. Unfortunately there is not (as yet) an agreed joint statistics form which can be used in all single congregation LEPs. At the time of writing, the Methodists and the United Reformed Church are piloting a type of joint form, but its success or otherwise has yet to be seen. Until then, you will need to complete yearly forms for each denomination. If you are a new church secretary it would be helpful to find out as soon as possible (either from the previous secretary or from the national denominational offices) what information you will need to give, so that you can keep correct records. This will usually include the number of infant baptisms, believers' baptisms, confirmations and funerals taking place in the church.

Child protection and 'Safe to Grow'

◆ Every church that has contact with children – on Sundays and/or midweek – needs to adopt a child protection policy. Full details of all that this involves as well as good practice guidelines and much more besides can be found in the BUGB publication *Safe to Grow*. Regular updates relating to Child Protection issues, including criminal records checks, are included in most issues of **Transform** which you will receive regularly.

◆ If your church doesn't have its own children's or youth work, but allows the premises to be used by others who do, then you should still have a child protection policy and also require that these other groups have policies that are consistent with yours.

◆ If your church doesn't have any contact with children or young people at the moment, it is possible that, at any time, a family arrives with children, or a local community group asks to use the premises for an activity involving children. It is better that a child protection policy is in place before this happens, rather than having to think through all of this at the last minute!

◆ The church leadership is responsible for making sure that a policy is in place and that it is both adhered to and updated as appropriate. Information about child protection issues and downloadable forms from the latest *Safe to Grow* book can be found on the BUGB website.

Congregational count

As part of the BUGB annual return form, churches are asked to conduct a congregational count on the first Sunday in December. This means that you need to count how many people are present at the main service that day – but you also need to know whether they are male or female and how old they are! Here are four possible ways of doing this.

◆ When you get home after the service make a list of all those who were present and what age group they fit into. (This only really works in small churches!)

◆ Have a volunteer stand at the door with a clipboard and paper divided into the appropriate number of sections. They then put a tick in the right section as each person enters. (This doesn't work well if you have a large number of people arriving at the last minute!)

◆ Hand out coloured slips of paper to everyone as they arrive (e.g. blue for men and pink for women) and then ask them to place these in one of five boxes. The boxes are labelled 'Aged under 14'; 'Aged 14–21'; 'Aged 22–50'; 'Aged 51–65'; 'Aged over 65'. Then all you have to do at the end is count the number of each colour in each box and enter those numbers on the form.

◆ During the service ask people to stand up if they fit into a certain category (e.g. men aged 22–50) and have someone count them. Given the date of the congregational count, it is possible to link this in with Mary and Joseph having to travel to Bethlehem for the census!

Constitution

◆ Every church should have a constitution which, in simple terms, is the formal way for stating how the church works. Its main purpose is to provide a framework for the organisation of church life. As such it needs to be clear and should not be in conflict with the laws of the country or older trust documents for your church which contain provisions that still apply.

◆ Eventually all churches will have to register with the Charity Commission and consequently will need constitutions that meet their criteria. If your church's constitution is quite old then this is a good time to introduce a new one. BUGB have produced a very helpful model constitution and this is contained in the BUC *Guideline* leaflet B9. This document is a good starting point which can be adapted to suit individual churches. The notes that accompany it indicate which are the clauses that need to be included to meet Charity Commission requirements.

◆ If you want to update your church's constitution then this is best done by a small group – such as a sub-group of the deacons. They can then present their work to the full diaconate (or other leadership group) before taking it to the church meeting. You will need to check your existing constitution as the procedure laid down for amending it will need to be followed. This will, almost certainly, require a Special Church Meeting and some considerable thought will need to go into the best way of presenting it to the members. A copy of your constitution should be sent to your holding trustees to make sure it doesn't conflict with your trust deeds.

Copyright and licences

◆ Copyright is the legal right of an author or composer to control the use of what he or she has written or created. Every piece of original work, whether written, composed or filmed, is protected by copyright during the creator's lifetime and for seventy years after the end of the year in which they died.

◆ To stay within the law, churches will need approval to photocopy hymns or songs or project them onto a screen, to photocopy music or text from books, to perform music in a concert or other non-service setting, to show videos or to use other people's work (writing and/or pictures) in a church magazine or on a website.

◆ To overcome the complexities involved in getting official approval every time you use a copyrighted resource in church, Christian Copyright Licensing International offers a set of simple licences. These licences are based on an annual fee which is tailored to the size of the congregation, and are designed to cover the various uses of material in different circumstances. To find out more visit www. ccli.co.uk or write to the address given in the resources chapter.

◆ Some service and prayer books allow you to reproduce the material for use within services without any further permission being needed. Look at the front of books you may want to copy to see what restrictions there are. For example, the BUGB *Gathering for Worship* book comes complete with a CD-Rom containing all the material in the book. The section 'Using this book' specifically says that most of the material in the book can be freely reproduced for local use.

◆ For more on this, and related issues, see BUC *Guideline* leaflet C10: *Licensing for Entertainment and Copyright*

Data Protection

◆ The Data Protection Act seeks to protect individuals against the unfair and unauthorised use of personal information. This means that, under the Act, individuals have a right to know what data is being held about them and be able to check its accuracy. There is also the need for those people and organisations who hold personal data to record such data only for the specific purposes for which it is held and only to disclose it to those authorised to have it.

◆ There are two issues for churches to be aware of. The first is the basic principles by which all data should be held and the second is whether the church needs to 'notify' (i.e. register with) the Office of the Information Commissioner.

◆ The Data Protection Act gives eight principles for dealing with personal data – whether kept on a computer or in a manual filing system. These are explained in the BUC *Guideline* leaflet C14: *Data Protection*. Churches should abide by these principles even if they do not have to notify.

◆ Churches processing personal data for usual church purposes (e.g. membership list) do not need to notify the Data Protection Registrar. If, however, data is held in connection with pastoral counselling or for fundraising purposes, then notification is required. For more information see the BUC *Guideline* leaflet or visit the Data Protection website www.informationcommissioner.gov.uk This includes a self-assessment guide to help individuals and organisations decide if they need to notify. Currently the notification charge is a £35 annual fee.

Disability Discrimination Act

◆ The 1996 Disability Discrimination Act means that it is unlawful for 'service providers' – which includes churches – to discriminate against people with a mental or physical disability. As a result many churches have made changes to their premises or to the services they offer to ensure that people of all abilities can participate as fully as possible. This has included installing suitable toilet facilities, installing an induction-loop system, providing large-print song-books and notice-sheets or using materials provided by BUild for people with learning difficulties.

◆ However, alongside any physical changes, there may also need to be changes in attitude! For example, church leaders and those who are part of the welcome team (or even the whole church) might like to consider disability awareness training such as that offered by the 'Through the Roof' organisation (www.throughtheroof.org). This website also contains a number of useful 'roofbreaker' guides on how to make your church welcoming to people with varying disabilities – at little or no cost. These include people with dyslexia, epilepsy and facial disfigurement as well as people with mobility or visual impairment.

◆ It is also a good idea to regularly review the church's activities to make sure that they really are accessible to people with disabilities.

◆ For more information obtain the BUC *Guideline* leaflet C13: *Disability Discrimination Act.*

Employment issues

◆ Churches appointing a minister are advised to use the recommended *Terms of Appointment* available from the Ministry Department of the Baptist Union.

◆ Churches employing non-ministerial staff – administrators, caretakers or youth workers for example – must comply with the complex requirements of employment law. If this is the case then the best advice I can give is to obtain a copy of the BUC *Guideline* leaflet C12: *Employment.* Employment legislation is constantly changing and evolving and this leaflet is frequently updated to take account of such changes. Ideally you should read this through before beginning any recruitment process.

◆ Some churches have been very surprised to find that they cannot automatically appoint a Baptist, or a Christian. The *Employment* leaflet gives details of the workbook *Christian Ethos Audit* that should also be reviewed before any recruitment process begins.

◆ Treasurers who join ACAT (Association of Church

Accountants and Treasurers) will find a very helpful section on employment issues included in the ACAT handbook.

Fire safety

See BUC *Guideline* leaflet C7: *Health and Safety and Fire Precautions.*

◆ As a result of the 'Regulatory Reform Fire Safety Order 2005' there is now a greater emphasis on fire prevention in non-domestic premises. The order requires fire precautions to be put in place 'where necessary' and to the extent that it is reasonable and practicable in the circumstances of the case. Responsibility for complying with the Fire Safety Order rests with the 'responsible person', which, in a church, will be the diaconate as a group. The 'responsible person' must carry out a fire risk assessment. Further information can be found in BUC *Guideline* leaflet C7 and at www.odpm.gov.uk where there is a guide to how this legislation affects 'places of assembly' (including churches).

◆ This risk assessment should cover: possible causes of fire; ways in which the risk of fire occurring and spreading can be minimized; means of fighting fire; fire detection and warning; emergency routes and exits; information on fire precautions; maintenance and testing of fire precautions.

First aid

See BUC *Guideline* leaflet C7: *Health and Safety and Fire Precautions.*

◆ Every church should have a suitably stocked first aid box and an appointed person to take charge of first aid arrangements.

◆ An appointed person is someone who takes charge when someone is injured or falls ill, including calling an ambulance if required, and who looks after the first aid equipment. They should not attempt to give first aid for which they have not been trained.

- You should put up a notice to say who the appointed person is and where the first aid box is kept. You may decide that you need more than the minimum first aid provision and that your appointed person should be a qualified first aider.

- The two main providers of first aid courses are the British Red Cross (www.redcrossfirstaidtraining.co.uk) and the St John Ambulance Brigade (www.sja.org.uk). This latter website also includes some useful downloadable first aid advice.

Food safety

See BUC *Guideline* leaflet C9: *Food Safety.*

- The Food Safety Act 1990 is the principal source of food safety law and provides wide ranging provisions which are aimed to strengthen and update the law on food safety and consumer protection.

- The *Guideline* leaflet provides a useful flow-chart to help you decide if your church needs to register with the Environmental Officer of your District Council. It certainly will need to do so if it regularly serves food and drink and stores food on the premises. Registration is free.

- Even if you don't need to register, the regulations relating to food safety and hygiene will apply to all church premises where food is served. It is a very good idea if the church has someone with overall responsibility for catering, and that they take a basic course in food hygiene. Details of courses can be obtained from your District Council.

- A very useful website which provides basic food safety and hygiene information can be found at www.foodlink. org.uk

Health and safety risk assessment

See BUC *Guideline* leaflet C7: *Health and Safety and Fire Precautions.*

◆ If you have at least one paid employee then you have a legal duty to assess the risks which exist on your premises and to reduce them as far as reasonably practicable.

◆ Even if you are not an employer, you may consider that you have a moral duty to your minister and to all those who use your premises to make them as safe as possible. (It is unclear as to whether a minister counts as an 'employee' in terms of Health and Safety legislation.)

◆ The *Guideline* leaflet includes advice on undertaking such a risk assessment and includes a very helpful checklist. It also includes a sample 'Health and Safety' policy which churches may wish to adapt for their own situation.

Vulnerable adults

◆ *Safe to Belong* is the name of the BUGB publication which includes guidelines and training material for churches working with vulnerable adults.

◆ The definition of a vulnerable adult is given by the government as someone 'who is or may be in need of community care services by reason of mental or other disability, of age or illness; and who is or may be unable to take care of him or herself, or unable to protect him or herself against significant harm or exploitation.'

◆ Many churches will have pastoral care teams visiting people who fall into this category and so it is important that churches make use of this material.

13

How to Cope with it All

This was a topic my husband said should be included! It is very easy to get so caught up with church life and its problems that your own health – spiritual, emotional, mental or physical – may be affected. It is important, therefore, to look after yourself and work out the best ways to cope.

In order to help write this chapter I asked some experienced church secretaries for their comments and so, with many thanks to Chris, Evelyn, John, Julie, Val and Wendy, here are some ideas which may be of help to you.

Delegate!

◆ I always feel a little hypocritical when speaking about this as I am probably the world's worst delegator! However, I have recognised over the years that it is something that church secretaries should do if at all possible.

◆ Very few people have the time and the gifting to do everything mentioned in this book and do it well. Most church secretaries will have other things in their life that have to be fitted in – such as a job and family commitments! So, be prepared to delegate tasks and to confess your difficulties and limitations.

◆ Too many church secretaries struggle on and on when they should be letting people help them. As one church secretary put it 'Delegate as much as you can and when people offer to help say "yes"'.

◆ Failing to delegate can deny other people an opportunity to use their God-given gifts to help others.

◆ And, as I explained in the introduction to this book, '… a church secretary is a facilitator – someone who enables things to happen, it doesn't mean they have to do everything themselves.'

Learn how to say no!

◆ This is really an extension of the above but it is important that you don't take on everything you are asked to do. There may well be others who can do a particular task as well as, or even better than, you can.

◆ It is also perfectly OK to admit there are things you don't know! Take advice from others, especially your regional ministers and other association or BUGB staff. (It is what they are there for!)

Have a good friend

◆ It is important that there is someone with whom you can share the joys and sorrows, the challenges and the frustrations of your role. This may be your husband or wife, your minister, another deacon or even someone from a different church.

◆ However it is vital that both of you know that what is said between you remains completely and absolutely confidential.

Be yourself

◆ Don't feel you have to be a clone of your predecessor – you will have different gifts and a different personality, so develop your own style.

◆ Don't feel you have to live up to other people's expectations. We are all human and can only do our best.

◆ Understand how you work best – if you are a planner, for example, then plan ahead – but also remember that not everyone works in this way.

◆ Work out the best way of remembering all you need to do. Some people love lists – others hate them! Discover what works best for you. For example, one church secretary has pieces of paper on his desk with different headings e.g. 'Deacons' Meeting', 'Church Meeting', 'Notice-sheet' and then whenever he thinks of something that needs to be remembered he writes it on the appropriate sheet. But this doesn't mean we should all do that!

I AM A VICTIM OF MY OWN ADMINISTRATION

Remember that you are more that the church secretary

- ◆ Develop a 'secretary's hat' that you can take off sometimes and just be yourself. For some this might mean not taking your diary to church on Sundays.

- ◆ Make time occasionally to worship elsewhere – it's a real pleasure to worship without having to think about who you need to talk to after the service!

- ◆ Attend association events and the Baptist Assembly – not just because you think you ought to, but with the anticipation of gaining something positive from the experience! Spiritual input from speakers, practical help from seminars and the opportunity to meet other Baptist Christians are some of the real positives!

- ◆ Don't feel guilty when you have to miss occasional Sundays due to family commitments or holidays!

- ◆ Take time to relax and get away from church life. For some people this means going swimming or walking or some other suitable form of enjoyable exercise! As well as the health benefits, you may also find this can be a time to think through issues that are concerning you.

- ◆ Try joining an organisation or group that has no church connection whatever! You may well find that a weekly night out with a totally different group of people and with no responsibilities can be very relaxing!

Don't let others upset you

- ◆ Easier said than done, but it is important not to take things too personally or take offence when people make critical comments, or appear to thwart your plans!

- ◆ Generally speaking, most people won't intentionally set out to annoy, irritate or upset you. If possible, try to understand where they are coming from and what is behind their comments and/or actions.

- ◆ Most people want to blame someone when things go wrong and the church secretary is often the one they choose. If this happens to you then make good use of your 'good friend' and also, if appropriate, talk about it with your minister or the rest of the leadership.

Prepare for your successor

- ◆ This shouldn't be a 'job for life' although for some people it does end up that way. (My own father was church secretary for nearly fifty years!)

- ◆ However long you have been doing the job, or think you might be doing the job, it is helpful to think of how you can prepare for someone else taking it on in the future. This might mean making notes about various aspects of things or keeping a loose-leaf folder with useful information in it. (Although this might not make your life easier, it will certainly help your successor!)

14
And Finally ...
Home Mission!

This book wouldn't exist without the help of Home Mission! This is because the association for which I work, and which allowed me the time to write this book, is funded by Home Mission. In addition many of the people who have helped me are also paid by Home Mission – colleagues in my own association, within other associations and at Baptist House.

What's more, without Home Mission, much of what is described within this book wouldn't exist as a free resource to Baptist churches. There would be no BUC *Guideline* leaflets, no National Settlement Team, no regional ministers, no help on child protection issues, no mission advisers ... freely available to you.

This is why it is important that all Baptist churches in membership of BUGB and/or one of the regional associations play their part in funding the wider Baptist family in England and Wales.

Many churches will do this through their church budget whilst others rely on individual donations from church members. (The best way is a combination of the two!) Some churches hold special fund-raising events, which can also be used to increase people's awareness of the wider Baptist family as well as providing opportunities for fellowship and fun.

The BUGB communications department produces a number of resources to help churches both promote and pray for the work of Home Mission – leaflets, magazines, the Prayer Guide, prayer-tapes (also available on CD and as audio files on the website), videos and DVDs, the website, posters and even an all-age worship pack. Encourage your church to make use of these resources.

Churches are encouraged to appoint Home Mission

representatives – people who could stimulate interest in, and support for, Home Mission. Home Mission representatives automatically receive promotional items throughout the year. More information about what is involved in this work can be found in the free leaflet 'Who'd be a Home Mission Representative' – available free from www.baptiststore.co.uk or from the BUGB communications department.

For more information on Home Mission see the relevant pages on the BUGB website.

15

Useful Resources

Websites

You will notice that I have made extensive use of websites in this book. This is because they are an excellent resource! Even if you don't have a computer with internet access there will probably be someone in your family or church who does have. In addition libraries will generally have computers that can be used free of charge and librarians to show you how to access the internet.

1. For updates to this book go to the relevant page on the BUGB website. If you find a web-link that is out of date or want to suggest a new resource that could be added to this website then contact me via this page. You will also find all web-links mentioned in this book on this page.

2. For news, information or help with anything Baptist then visit www.baptist.org.uk. On this website you will find, amongst other things, the whole range of BUC *Guideline* leaflets and a link to www.baptiststore.co.uk from where you can order many BUGB publications. The website also has pages giving contact details and website links for all the regional associations and Baptist colleges in membership with BUGB.

3. The best website that I have found relating to church administration is www.john-truscott.co.uk. John is a church consultant and trainer who is 'committed to helping churches and mission agencies become effective in Christian service.' His website includes a number of downloadable resources which can be reproduced (maximum thirty copies) for use within your church. I have made reference to a number of these throughout the book as they are free resources that may be of help to a number of churches. John also runs training events and

a consultancy programme – details of which are also on the website.

4. A couple of websites which give advice on creating a church website are www.church123.com – click on 'Hints and Tips' and www.cofeguildford.org.uk/html/resources/web-creation/website.shtml – a useful downloadable booklet produced by the communications department of Guildford Diocese is available here. In addition, John Truscott has an article on the subject on his website.

5. Other websites which might be of interest.

www.acat.uk.com – the website of the Association of Church Accountants and Treasurers. All treasurers are encouraged to join ACAT and details of how to do this can be found on this website.

www.bedyddwyr-baptistwales.co.uk – the website for the Baptist Union of Wales (under construction at time of writing).

www.bmsworldmission.org – the website for BMS World Mission.

www.cartoonchurch.com – a good source of cartoons about church life.

www.ccli.co.uk – for anything to do with copyright issues in churches. The website includes the useful downloadable 'AB© of Copyright'.

www.charity-commission.gov.uk – the website of the Charity Commission.

www.foodlink.org.uk – a very useful website providing basic food safety and hygiene information.

www.dwp.gov.uk/resourcecentre/social_fund.asp – to download leaflets about what to do after a death (D49 or D49S).

www.gro.gov.uk – the website for the General Register Office. Provides information about the legal aspects of getting married as well as links to all local Register Offices.

www.informationcommissioner.gov.uk – the Data Protection website. This will help you find out if you need to 'notify' (register) and also provides an online notification facility.

www.parishpump.co.uk – a useful resource site for church magazine editors. Every month they produce graphics, news, stories, children's pages, puzzles, magazine covers, reviews, cartoons, quotes, jokes, prayers and poems – which can be downloaded by members. There is an annual fee but you can have a month's free membership to enable you to sample their material.

www.redcrossfirstaidtraining.co.uk – details of first aid and health and safety training courses run by the Red Cross in your area.

www.scottishbaptist.org.uk – the website for the Baptist Union of Scotland.

www.sja.org.uk – useful downloadable advice on basic first aid as well as details of courses run by the St John Ambulance Brigade.

www.themarriagecourse.org – details of marriage courses from the home of the Alpha Course.

www.throughtheroof.org – provides online help and advice and a selection of resources to buy on the subject of making our churches accessible to all – and not just in the physical sense. The organisation also runs 'open church workshops' for churches.

www.videolicence.co.uk – the website where you can buy a licence for videoing a wedding.

Books and leaflets

The following publications relate in some way to church life. Unless indicated otherwise they have been published by BUGB and are available from them.

Baptism and Belonging by Rob Warner is a helpful booklet for people considering baptism and church membership.

Beyond the OHP by Jackie Sheppard (published by Spring Harvest but available from BUGB Publications). A practical introduction and guide to using technology in worship.

BUC *Guideline* leaflets available on a wide range of practical, financial and legal issues. These can be downloaded from www. baptist.org.uk/resources/guidelines.htm or ordered from the BUC office at Baptist House.

Christian Ethos Audit packs have been developed by Faithworks in conjunction with BUGB to help churches and Christian organisations understand the new employment legislation and implement necessary changes to their employment practices. They can also be obtained from the Faithworks website www.faithworks.info.

Facing a Pastoral Vacancy – the guide for churches who are facing a pastoral vacancy!

Gathering for Worship edited by Chris Ellis and Myra Blyth contains service outlines, prayers and other resources for people leading worship. It comes with a free CD containing all the material in the book, allowing you to edit it for your own use. Patterns and prayers for all kinds of services are included along with guidelines and reflections to help both new and experienced worship leaders.

Getting the Message Across by Richard Littledale. Although technology has moved on since this was written it is still a very useful guide for anyone producing church newsletters, magazines and/or notice-sheets.

How to be Heard in a Noisy World – a comprehensive guide to Christian publicity by Phil Creighton. (To be published by Authentic Media in November 2006.)

Radical Believers by Paul Beasley-Murray A very helpful book for those who want to think through the 'Baptist way of being church'.

Radical Leaders by Paul Beasley-Murray – the book that, in my view, should be read and discussed by elders and deacons (and their equivalents) in all our churches!

Safe to Grow – guidelines on child protection for the local church and its youth leaders.

Who'd be a Baptist? – a free leaflet which gives a useful introduction to Baptist life.

Other

Fit4*Life* is a CD-based resource developed by Australian Baptists and is designed to help churches behave well and develop healthy practices. The course contains numerous practical exercises for group work and covers topics such as communication, handling differences, decision-making and clarifying role expectations. It is available from the Anabaptist Network and, currently costs £10. For more details go to www.anabaptistnetwork.com/node/234 or write to Anabaptist Network, 14 Shepherds Hill, London N6 5AQ.

Contact details

The Baptist Union of Great Britain
www.baptist.org.uk
Baptist House, PO Box 44, 129 Broadway, Didcot, Oxfordshire OX11 8RT
Tel: 01235 517700
E-mail: info@baptist.org.uk

Baptist Union of Scotland
www.scottishbaptist.org.uk
Resource House, 14 Aytoun Road, Pollockshields, Glasgow G41 5RT
Tel: 0141 423 6169
E-mail: admin@scottishbaptist.org

Baptist Union of Wales
www.bedyddwyr-baptistwales.co.uk
Ilston House, 94 Mansel Street, Swansea SA1 5TZ
Tel: 01792 655 468

BMS World Mission
www.bmsworldmisison.org
Baptist House, PO Box 49, 129 Broadway, Didcot, Oxfordshire OX11 8XA
Tel: 01235 517700
E-mail: mail@bmsworldmission.org

The Charity Commission
www.charity-commission.gov.uk
For all general Charity Commission enquiries, call their contact centre – 0845 300 0218
The contact centre is open 08.30 until 18.00, Monday to Friday.

Advisors are available to answer all general enquiries to the Commission, offering advice on a wide range of issues.
E-mail enquiries should be sent to enquiries@charitycommission.gsi.gov.uk
The address for written enquires varies as different offices handle different regions and size of charity. Details can be obtained from the website or the contact centre number given above.

CCLI Ltd
www.ccli.co.uk
PO Box 1339, Eastbourne, East Sussex BN21 1AD
Tel: 01323 417711
E-mail: admin@ccli.org.uk
For all enquiries relating to copyright issues and licences (including video licences).

Christian Deaf Link UK
www.deafchristian.org.uk
Friendship House, 484 Southchurch Road, Southend on Sea, Essex SS1 2QA
Minicom: 01702 613114
Tel/fax: 01702 613113
Email: general@christiandeaflink.org.uk
An organisation aiming to meet the social and spiritual needs of deaf people through innovative Christian work.

Torch Trust for the Blind
www.torchtrust.org
Torch House, Torch Way, Northampton Road, Market Harborough, Leicestershire LE16 9HL
Tel: 01858 438260
E-mail: info@torchtrust.org
The Torch Trust produces Christian literature in formats that blind and partially sighted people can read, and promotes Christian fellowship with and among blind and partially sighted people.

Index